WHEN JESUS ISN'T ENOUGH

Monica Matthews is living proof that **God uses our life struggles to create sparkling diamonds.** If you've ever felt discouraged, empty, or alone as a Christian woman, let *When Jesus Isn't Enough* fill you up and encourage you to live in the freedom only Christ can bring. **Monica's new book is a deeply satisfying read for every Christian woman!**

JACI VELASQUEZ
Dove Award-Winning Singer, Songwriter, Actress and Author

Quick witted, strong, courageous, and authentic—get ready to go behind the scenes of Monica's journey that will inspire and give hope to many. You'll learn the source of her true identity as she challenges you to dig a little deeper in your own journey of life.

SHANNEN FIELDS
Actress, *Facing the Giants*, Speaker, Producer

Monica Matthews is a force of brutal honesty. With this offering—her labor of love for her Triune-God—she invites you to bring your hungry heart to the table and be fed. *Bon appetit!*

BEN CHAMBERS
Director of Young Life USC/UCLA

As a widow of 17 years and a self-proclaimed woman at the well who has experienced the demons of singleness from poverty to loneliness, Monica candidly evaluates the plight of single women and invites them to feast at the table of Jesus, and see that He truly is enough. **This is a powerful and inspiring read for every single woman.**

GINNY DENT BRANT
Speaker, Author of *Finding True Freedom: From the White House to the World*

Monica Matthews brings a lifetime of faith, moxie and experience to everything she does. From her weekly talk show to her ministry to her music and writing, **Monica always delivers an entertaining—and inspirational—outlook on life and faith.** There's always an opportunity to laugh, cry, respond, and even take notes every time.

SCOTT SLADE
Host of *Atlanta's Morning News*

Monica Matthews is an inspiration not only to single or widowed women, but to married women, as well. In *When Jesus Isn't Enough*, she speaks with such eloquence and rawness at the same time. **If you're looking for a 'sugar coated' book this is not for you. Monica is real and doesn't add 'fluff' to who she is or her story.** She shares her experiences in a biblically solid way that spotlights the pure gospel. *When Jesus Isn't Enough* **is a book everyone should read!**"

SHERYL GRIFFIN
Author and Speaker

Monica shares openly and honestly about her life and journey to Christ. Her 'revelatory hope' shared throughout her story will give a renewed resolve to follow God. Monica's easy-to-read style is candid and transparent yet convicting--as she points women towards Jesus Christ. **Her message for men is much needed, too—to live responsibly, in honor, and with accountability.**

TIM ECHOLS
Georgia Public Service Commissioner, Minister, Author, and Founder of Teen-Pact Leadership School.

Tired of faking it? Monica delivers **a refreshing, candid read for anyone who's ever felt like there must be more to faith and life** than the platitudes and cliches we often hear in church. Read this book now for an inspirational meal that will leave you focused on the One who brings true satisfaction!

BILL BLANKSCHAEN
FaithWalkers.com, Author of *A Story Worth Telling*
and Co-author of *You Will Be Made to Care*

WHEN JESUS **ISN'T** ENOUGH

WHEN *Jesus* **ISN'T** ENOUGH

The Ultimate Meal for the Starving Single Woman

MONICA
MATTHEWS

Published by StoryBuilders
MyStoryBuilders.com
in partnership with
Monica Matthews
Atlanta, Georgia, U.S.A.
MonicaMatthews.com
Printed in the U.S.A.

Photos of Monica Matthews by Mia McCorkle, JTM Photography, Atlanta

To purchase additional copies of this book,
visit MonicaMatthews.com, call 855-932-7749,
or email enough@monicamatthews.com

I DEDICATE THIS COMPLETED BODY OF WORK TO

THE MAN I LOVE: MY FATHER, JOHN G. MARINOS,

THE ONE WHO GAVE ME A NAME, A HERITAGE, AND A LEGACY

AND WHO ALWAYS MADE FOOD, AND LIFE, ABOUT

love

I DID IT, DADDY!

I remember a particular relationship to which I had made a vow in my heart and mind, even to my heavenly Dad. When the man said goodbye, I became the woman at the well, adorned by guilt and pain and in my gown of shame with a broken heart and torn clothing.

Thankfully, Jesus met me and offered me His cup of salvation once again (see Ps. 116:13). I could have argued as I had in the past that I wasn't worthy—But this time I didn't.

I didn't run to my usual comforts: excessive first dates, flirting, becoming a super religious nun chick, ordering a lock for my chastity belt, beating myself up day and night with guilt, overeating, drinking, becoming social queen of the month or supermom of the year. I no longer had the strength for all that.

I was spiritually, emotionally, and physically dehydrated. I too have been blind, willful, stubborn, beguiled, naked, and left for dead. Raped by the enemy of my soul (satan) and my agreements with him.

Repent, sweet babies. Repent. "He is faithful and just to forgive us our sins, and to cleanse us from unrighteousness" (1 John 1:9). That's love. Love covers (see Gen. 3:21; 1 Pet. 4:8).

XO

Monica

Contents

Aperitif

Fine Dining:
True Comfort Food

As a widowed woman of seventeen years (who spent her entire thirties alone), if I've heard one well-meaning married woman tell me that Jesus should be enough for me, I've heard a thousand. In the frustration of those incessantly annoying "We don't really know why you're still single, but hang in there, girl" or "Maybe if you just jump through enough hoops, God will bless you" answers, I decided to write about this Jesus-being-enough business. Because honestly, many times I found myself starving and thirsting in loneliness, making comparisons and feeling frustration as a single woman. In those moments I decided that Jesus wasn't enough, and I indulged in buffets that left me even more weary, famished, and dehydrated.

"Buffets?" you ask? Let me explain.

My daughter and I, in one of our many discussions about this Christianity thing, realized one night that our relationship with Jesus seems at times much like experiences we've had at fine dining establishments or at wedding celebrations. We walk in *starving* and parched only to look down at the finely designed but meager-looking meal on our plates and think, *really? This is supposed to satisfy our hunger and thirst?* Yet in the end we realize that it was not only exactly what we needed—it was more than enough! (This illustration is how my daughter came to be the mental creative force behind our delicious-looking cover.)

And I have come to find out that Jesus is more than enough. As I wrote this book—actually, prepared this fine dining experience for you—I tasted a Savior and friend with arms wide open waiting to address my needs as a woman, right where I'm at. He can do the same for you.

The problem is that we Americans are so accustomed to an abundance of food—and easy food. Our waistlines, diseases, and ineffective spirituality speak to our buffet mentality. We pick and choose and think more and bigger are better. But quality doesn't always equal quantity. Whether we eat a legitimate meal or a spiritual one, many of us are simply engorged, bloated with sugary carbs that give us short bursts of energy but no lasting stamina. The fillers. Ultimately, these leave us exhausted, physically and otherwise.

But fine dining is not about glutting ourselves. The entire experience of dining is a celebration of life, from the chef who painstakingly envisions and prepares it, seeing to every detail, to the one who humbly serves it to our little hungry tummies. While the cost for a lavish meal is hardly menial, the reward is exponential on so many levels. We leave satisfied, nourished, comforted and replenished. We have been served *with* life to *sustain* life.

This book, ladies, is about fine dining. Nourishment. Comfort. And fellowship with other women who walk in your shoes.

So welcome! I am so glad you are joining us—my Dad (God the Father), my Fiancé (Jesus), the Holy Spirit, and me—for a delicious health-conscious meal!

Partaking of This Fine-Dining Experience

Many times we ask, what is God's will for my life? Well here it is, both corporately and individually: that we repent from dead works, be restored to who we are in righteousness, peace, and joy—and then nourish others in the body of Christ so they can do the same. We are not autonomous. We are a living, breathing, moving organism called the church (see 1 Cor. 12:12). For that reason I encourage you to share this meal with a group of friends.

It's okay to eat it alone too—you'll still be nourished and comforted. But it's my hope that in reading this book with your sisters, they will come alongside you to honor you and glorify God's workmanship in you and that you will do the same for others. I desire that you partner with each other and commit to running your race together with integrity and transparency—because I'm doing that with *you*. I'm here. Raw, honest, and gratefully filled with hope that *freedom* will prevail on these pages. Let your yes be yes and your no, no with each other. See in every sister a glimpse of yourself, and cover her with honesty, mercy and love.

Scriptural Truth

I have settled it in my heart and bones that the book we call the Bible encompasses the Spirit and soul of our Father God and our Fiancé, Jesus, inerrantly. Not only do I accept this as truth by faith and spirit, but the logical, ever-intellectual side of my being reasons that a book containing three languages, written over three continents by over forty authors in sixty-six books over a span of fifteen hundred years, and packed with fulfilled Scriptural prophecy is enough succinct literary cohesion for me to say yes to its truth.

They (the Godhead) have a lot to say to us about ourselves—not only as daughters and heirs but as single chicks in this day and age—and Their book is not as "religious" as you might think. We have a place at our Father's table, since as single ladies, we live in our Father's house and are under His protection.

While God can meet you in whichever version of the Bible you feed from, this meal will simply not taste the same if not consumed with the King James Version in hand. (Think of it as not using your mama's ingredients yet expecting your meal to taste *exactly* like hers).

As a writer, words are the ingredients with which I prepared my meal. They matter. I chose them carefully and weighed them in precision so that they would rise and serve you in the most nourishing way. If the KJV is intimidating for you due to the "thee" and "thou" issue, I highly encourage you to sit with your preferred version along with a KJV so that you can receive the full heart and nutritional benefit of this meal.

Three in One

We welcome you to our meal—my Dad, my Fiancé, His Holy Spirit, and me! For the purposes of this meal, I refer to the Godhead not only as I experience Them personally but also as They describe Themselves.

Jesus is Lord, and I accept Him as such. But I've witnessed what I refer to as Jesus "idolatry," which excludes our Father. Opposed to proper worship and adoration, doing this leaves out an essential ingredient in the completion of our meal, our Father God, as if Jesus were the only person in the Godhead. When we do this, we remain spiritual orphans. This is not His/Their will for us. We are daughters of our Father.

Our Father and His Son, along with God's powerful Spirit, who inhabits our bodies as His temple, make up one fantastically incomparable meal referred to as the Godhead. To avoid sparking theological debate, I am simply clueing you in as to why I refer to Them in a unified yet individual manner throughout this meal: we can't afford to leave any of Them out (see Gen. 1:26; Acts 17:29; Rom. 1:20; Col. 2:9)!

A Slow Cooker

I designed this meal for you to take time to savor each bite and to digest it for the best assimilation. Nine courses (plus dessert!) may seem like an eternity for those of you who, like myself, want to race through most things, including what matters most: our time with God and ourselves. But I encourage you to commit this time to yourself, to your Maker, and to the generations that will follow you.

When you arrive at the end of this meal, whether you have partaken of it alone or in a group, I encourage you to seal your courage, commitment, and completion of your time here by celebrating with a home-cooked meal. In this way you can give *God* the glory for all He's brought you through, and He can glory in *you*. Breaking bread, especially with others who share your joy, provides a powerful time of fellowship and something that our kingdom takes seriously!

Cleansing Your Palate

In every fine meal, prior to moving on to the next course, it is suggested that one wash the palate to ensure the full measure of taste and enjoyment for the next course. You will have the opportunity to do just that at the end of each course. This is where you will take what you have just read and spend some time feeding on Jesus for yourself.

You'll do this by looking at His Word and allowing Him to speak to your heart Himself. Being Berean—checking out the Scriptures on your own to be sure of their truth (see Acts 17:10-11)—is a must in this day and age.

You'll also have a chance to answer some honest "get real" questions that you will hopefully answer with absolute transparency. Whether you are studying alone or with a group, this can seem scary, but the good news is, He (They—the Godhead) already know your answers! And facing them brings you to a place where you can find healing.

This isn't just my story. It's quite possibly yours. I would hate for you to miss the salt—the Word of God and your own personal time with Jesus—that was used to flavor this meal meant to nourish and replenish the cells of your heart.

Scraps Are for Dogs

Jesus, the lamb, was prepared for us—His body broken and His blood spilled for us, His girls—so that He could buy us back from the one

I refer to as the pimp of the universe. From the one ever selling us downstream to a gruesome end. I'm thinking that it's time we quit eating scraps from the "everything you shouldn't eat" buffet and pull up a chair, even with all our "stuff," and sup with the One who is the only meal that will ever truly satisfy us.

I'm proud to introduce my Fiancé, and I'm learning to accept that He is proud of me too, flaws and all. After all, as my pastor reminds me, "I'm just a girl"—*His* girl. I pray that this meal is refreshing for your soul and as helpful to your mind as it has been for me and mine to say yes to His pursuit of me—again. Not only as God's daughter but as His fiancée, a bride in the making.

I am writing to you in the hopes that you won't feel alone and forgotten. You are not. *We* are not (see Heb. 13:5). I minister to many women who feel and believe otherwise.

As of the publishing of this book, I'm not a married woman who has a man's warm body, an earthly covering, a life companion, a fellow visionary—also known as a husband—telling unmarried women how to live in contentment as a single, godly woman. I'm not offering a magical formulaic expression or five steps to figuring out how to get God to unleash your Boaz from the heavenlies (check out the book of Ruth). No. I'm your single sister who is personally fed up with believing the lie of the enemy of our souls (see Eph. 6:12) that because I am a single woman, something is wrong with me, men, or God—and that for some reason I need to wait to *live*. I've simply grown weary of not believing and living the truth that Jesus *really is enough*.

Bon appétit!
XO,
Your sister in Christ,
Mon

Acknowledgments

I would like to thank my earthly father for always encouraging me to finish what I started. For crediting what he admired about me to "being a Christian woman." Thank you for trusting me with your heart and allowing me to pour into you and honor you as a daughter should. Thank you for providing for me, always, and for claiming me when no one else would.

I thank my mother for her courage to travel the seas and come to an unknown country to begin an epic journey of life. Thank you for encouraging me to be strong and to make my house a home. Thank you for teaching me that beauty is to be cared for and how to be a lady.

A special thanks to my Bean for your unconditional love and acceptance. Thank you for never giving up and for your undying honor of me as your mother. Thank you for always being teachable and giving me many years of laughter, tears, dreams, and amazing conversation. I'm at least forty years smarter because of you.

Thank you to my pastors and ministers who have provided countless hours of shoulder time for tears and bear hugs. Thank you for ministering to my broken heart and being Jesus to me on so many levels. You make me proud to be part of the body of Christ. I would not be the woman I am today without each of you.

My friends and enemies receive an equal amount of gratitude. My life has been enriched greatly by all of you. I've learned to love and exercise my faith, thanks to all of you, and to be tenacious and never give up due to the countless hours my friends have spent listening to my doubts, fears, frustrations, and hopes and the moments of utter despair and great breakthrough joy.

I'd also like to thank Becky, the world's most patient and dedicated editor! You made me think and feel and go to the uncomfortable transparent places so that others could join me. Thank you for helping me shape and tell my story. Thank you for your excellence and mercy. I learned a lot.

My thanks for the photo of the scrumptious, conservative (by American all-you-can-eat standards) yet costly meal featured on the cover, which was prepared by my dear childhood friend and internationally respected chef Pano Karatassos.

Last and never least, my heavenly family. Holy Spirit, I apologize for grieving You with many silly decisions and agreements with our enemy. I thank You for whispering to me and taking up residence in me when I thought I was a tomb. Thank You for comforting me and leading me into all discernment.

Thank you, Jesus, for being everything. Just everything. That by Your word the sun I love so much rises and sets. That the birds I hear can sing because You gave them a melody. That the air I breathe is because You blew across space and time to breathe life into an otherwise desolate existence. Thank You for raising me from the dead and for being a very present help in times of trouble. Thank You for being my friend and advocate, my Savior.

And Father, what can I say? You've endured the most. Thank You for sending Your Son here to serve me in ways I could never repay. Thank You for listening, instructing, correcting, and walking with me on my lonely paths and my crowded ones. Thank You for visiting me when I was in my self-made prison and when my bed was in hell. Thank You that You are greater than any meme we could create to box You into a human narrative. Thank you for Your truth and wisdom. Thank You, above all, for Your forgiveness and faithfulness. Thank You for the freedom You brought me through your Son and for redeeming me as Your beloved daughter.

Shaped by Abuse—
But God

Little bag in hand, I began the looming climb up the red brick steps—that ominous staircase to the entryway of an old, musty, downtown Atlanta house. I hated this place. It scared me. She, the mean one, watched me. I didn't know her. I didn't understand why I was staying here. Mommy had to work. It was night when I arrived and night when I left. I wasn't safe. Mommy didn't know.

I felt his hands. I felt his breath on the side of my face. I lay there and didn't move. I was frozen. I wanted my mommy. Where was my mommy? Why was he touching me? It was cold. I had nothing to cover myself with. I wasn't safe. Mommy had no idea what was happening. Neither did I. I was only three.

I felt his hands. I felt his breath on the side of my face. I lay there and didn't move. I was frozen. I wanted my mom. Where was my mom? Why was he touching me? I wasn't safe. I was only thirteen.

I felt his hand across my mouth. I was asleep. I was drunk. I was minding my own business in my own bed. I saw his face. I heard his threatening voice. I smelled the stench of his self-absorbed power. I felt him take what wasn't his and was never mine. I felt everything and nothing. I didn't want my mom. I didn't want anyone. It was probably my fault—again. I wasn't safe. I was only twenty.

Disillusioned

I was married for a very brief moment in time.

We met on a lively dance-club floor in an Atlanta hotspot. We had mutual friends, and the chase began almost instantly.

We quickly moved in together and a year later bought our first home. I wanted a wedding before a house, but my then boyfriend had other ideas. We had money for a house or a wedding but not both. My family wouldn't pay for my wedding, because my man didn't "look" like us. It was rough.

A few months after moving into our new home, my little Bean planted herself on my uterine wall. I could tell you the exact night she was conceived. To say that I was scared would be an understatement. My husband was completely fine with it and shouted, "We're gonna have a baby!" I was still scared.

Here I was at twenty-four, while my father hated my choice for a mate, I had no ring (but I did have a shared mortgage), with my whole life seeming to close in on me with those two little stripes on a stick.

This even though a few short weeks prior to God sending my little one to earth, I had cooed and awed over every child that had come to our door for Halloween. My ovaries were screaming, "*Child! We want a baby!*" This was the first time I became hyper-aware of my intention to be a mother. I wanted one of those little creatures more than anything.

Still, I was terrified at the prospect of giving up my life for someone else to that extent, and I was genuinely scared about what having a child would mean for my life as I knew it. Nothing was happening in the order I had always dreamed of, and although I wasn't yet born again, my heart yearned for the appropriate order of things in life. On some level I resigned myself to the fact that life just wasn't going to work out in order, and I did what I always do—I lived to the fullest.

We married just a few short months after our birth announcement, and shortly thereafter, we both lost our jobs. Life got real interesting. I watched my husband pound the pavement until his spirit was completely beaten down. Eventually he turned to a 100 percent commission job, and *we* quickly became *I*.

My young husband began to turn to many things besides our marriage for comfort, and I found myself alone, angry, and hurt. I was pregnant, jobless, and lonely. We were both young, inexperienced in anything selfless, as it were, and scared to death about our future. We had no God, no money, no prospects, and our love was somewhere on the back burner. But Bean.

My Bean and I became inseparable. You may be thinking, *Well, duh—you were pregnant!* But this was a different kind of inseparable. She became my best friend. From her safe place inside me, she listened to my woes and heard my tears. She was a precious thing for me to protect at all costs. I couldn't protect her, though, from my feelings of despair and isolation. She and I paid for that later. Our babies feel everything; every chemical that runs through our pregnant veins runs a direct course to their ever-evolving being.

As her birth approached, I found employment at a local deli that a friend owned and began the nesting process. My husband was MIA and in complete despair, since the commission job hadn't panned out. I did what any wife worth her office would do and wrote and submitted his resume, without his knowledge, to everyone in his industry. All I knew was that I had a human being on the way who would need care, shelter, food, and a lot of diapers—and sitting around feeling sorry for ourselves wasn't going to satisfy any those needs.

The day Bean was born, he received a call from an employer that he couldn't have imagined. The company, in need of his expertise and offering full benefits, offered him a professional home. A blessing. By this time we had also had a come-to-Jesus moment with my father, and my father officially accepted my husband as his son-in-law, as my husband and the father of Papou's little angel. God was faithful. My father never really forgave himself for not attending my wedding and for holding on to his long-held beliefs regarding race mingling. It broke my heart. I pray that Jesus has given him rest in his soul regarding that period. I forgave him moons ago.

Just shy of Bean's first birthday, my husband noticed the first symptom of a disease that would take us through a valley we could not have foreseen, much less prepared for.

Upon further investigation, and two quarters into my return to college, he was diagnosed with motor neuron disease. Well, that was great, but we had no idea what it meant. We had no idea that within two months he would never walk again or hold his daughter. We had no idea that I would lay next to his hospital bed in our den, not sleeping for four days at a time to make sure he was still breathing, and feed him the same food I was feeding our one-year-old. No idea that just a month later, when I was twenty-six years of age, I would have to decide whether to place him on life support or let him go. A real-time nightmare.

The next two years encompassed a ride of epic proportion. We had no idea what he was truly ill with, and as the process of elimination and various treatments failed, I watched a 220-pound, full-of-life athlete at the top of his game whither away to 130 pounds. He had zero ability to speak or to move a single muscle in his body—not even his eyes. It was truly unreal. I would not wish this disease on my worst enemy.

In the end, we never truly knew what took his life. Through the grim process of an autopsy, it was reported that it was most closely linked to ALS.

Shattered

I watched him die a slow, grueling death. I buried him. He was thirty-three. I was left with a three-year-old daughter, a broken heart, shattered dreams, fear, and the reality of my so-called life. I never finished that college degree, because I was caring for him. I had no plans. Only a voice to sing with—but I couldn't breathe. I wasn't safe. I was only twenty-eight.

During the two years of his illness, things had emerged that changed my heart and my head for a very long time. Things about trust, commitment, and the necessity to desire God.

My life took a turn that no one could have seen coming, particularly me. I became a woman of scorn, loss, and hopelessness. I turned back to what I knew: music and the world. I ran like crazy so I could live and not die with my husband. I wish I could tell you that my daughter was my inspiration for living, but not dying was my inspiration for living.

The scene of my husband's weakness coupled with the trauma of indiscretions was too much for me, and I became a Rahab of epic proportions.

Staring at my watch one morning, I wondered when the guy beside me would wake up and get out of my bed so I could get on with my day and fill my wounds with another one. I had decided, "If this is all I'm worth, then this is what I'll give. I will become like my enemy and better. I will eat men for lunch and spit them out for dinner."

I took every assault, every betrayal, every taking of my innocence, trust, and safety, and I asserted my hatred of men with the very body they all craved. I became harder than my enemy, and I sought to destroy them, one by one.

I gave what I wanted, when I wanted, to whom I wanted. I died, with my enemy, in the mirror of lies of a life gone horribly wrong from the beginning. I betrayed myself, because I no longer mattered. Neither did they. I was dead. I was only twenty-nine.

Alive

Staring one morning into the blue eyes of a soul that no longer breathed, I didn't know who I was. I was gone. A shell of a woman, I was worse than lost. I had become a beautiful corpse. I said to a God I didn't know, "If You are real, show up now, please, because I can't go on another day this way." I fell to my bedroom floor in a fetal position and wept for hours. I was beyond crushed. I had no soul. I had given away all that was left from my childhood. I was nothing.

He responded. I was only twenty-nine.

That day birthed my love for Jesus Christ and opened the Scriptures to my understanding and my heart. I devoured the meal of His Word for two weeks without leaving my home, answering a phone, even eating. My daughter was with my parents, and I literally sat at the feet of Christ and fed from His hand with a hunger and a thirst that I had never known.

Finally, beyond satisfied, nourished, and filled with hope and forgiveness, I realized for the first time in my life that I was clean. I was loved. I was accepted, and I was known. I was forgiven, and I mattered. My life was never the same.

Coming to Christ helped me realize that my husband had been human and young and without God's input in life and in our marriage. We had both lacked the tools of Christ to make the kind of marriage that God longs for two people in covenant to share. We'd had ideas and long-held stories of what marriage could or should look like, but the breath of God had been void from our union. Through the revelation of Christ, I forgave him through Christ's eyes, and I forgave myself. The Lord restored my hope in marriage and, more importantly, my hope in life and love.

A few short weeks after my healing began, I made my first trip to Los Angeles for vocal training, and I had the spiritual honeymoon of a lifetime. I saw Him in everything. I saw His majesty in the canyons and in the coastline, and in every person I encountered, I saw His beauty and breath. I was alive. Fully alive.

Shortly after meeting my heavenly Father in such an epic way, I discovered that all my inheritance was gone. Unknowingly, I had trusted a con and invested in payphones directly before the cellphone boom. Yep. Broke, widowed, raising a daughter, I set my face like flint and proceeded onto a path that I thought would continue to be a straight and narrow honeymoon with Jesus. That was just the beginning. I was only thirty.

Standing, Running, Flying

I did it. I raised her. A brilliant eighteen-year-old young woman, she was now off to one of the greatest educational campuses in the US. From the devouring of my soul to my saying yes to Christ to this very moment, I have lived a life worth sharing, for one reason: His glory. I'm only forty-five.

My dawning awareness of who I had become put me gently on the path of the book you are holding in your hands. To write it all down I've had to muster up some serious courage and trust and then venture into the caverns of my life. I had to allow Him to shine a light on those unseen things that create life less abundant in patterns of worry, dissatisfaction, striving, and insecurity, to name a few.

Are the scenes above told by countless others? Yes. Are they worthy of pity? No. Are they redemptive? Absolutely. I wish I could tell you that Jesus has been my all in all through the past seventeen years of widowhood. That I've been celibate, clean, pure, and filled with holiness and that my life as a single Christian woman has been all rainbows and unicorns. But I'd be lying.

On the contrary, it's been messy, downright ghastly, pathetic, sad—and yet redemptive. I've gone back to my vomit as the dog, I've left my first love, I've waited and not waited, I've been washed only to dirty myself again. I've sought God, and I've said "Forget You" to God and His righteous kingdom after finding them. I've asked, "Where the heck were You when I was three and violated?! Where were You when I was taken by the enemy and used for his purposes? Where were You when I shared the only thing that seemed of worth with men I encountered in the hopes of finding acceptance and safety?"

I've hated myself and others. I've warred with a devil who not only worked through others to destroy me at an early age but trained me to agree with self-destructive and generational patterns that led me to horrific decisions in life. He slammed me on every mountaintop of sanctification and every valley of abject human loneliness. He worked overtime to cause me to doubt that I am actually a redeemed daughter of Someone who will never betray me, who loves me unconditionally, and who can and will wash me and train me in the ways of life more abundant. He whispers to me still, through my continued struggle with sin, that I am altogether incapable of willful obedience and must simply not love God enough. Or worse, he tells me that somehow sin doesn't equal death, because God's grace covers it anyway. He likes to take my eyes back to the past and glue my wings to it as if the blood shed for my perpetrators and for me isn't enough. He longs to write the final chapter in my book of life. But he's a liar.

I'm not a victim. I am "just" a girl. I am made up of many things, but I am not the sum total of my moments, because I am still growing and receiving. I am still standing, and I plan to run. I am mounting up my wings as an eagle, and I want to share my journey, because it's vast and not over and because I've found through the past seven years of ministry that my story is similar to those of many others. Our Father is faithful, and what He has done, is doing, and will do for me, He will do for you. My life is living proof of Romans 8:28: "We know that all things work together for good to them that love God, to them who are the called according to his purpose."

Even though He made me a new creation, I still struggle. I still feel as if He's not enough sometimes. I felt it especially on those nights when I almost lost my only child to a chronic illness that plagued our home for nearly eleven years. And on those days and nights I *felt* so alone in this thing called life. Oh, but He is enough. He truly is all I need. He *is* the hero I've always desired.

I'm inviting you into our story, hoping that perhaps you will open your heart to endless possibilities of your own. My wounds and my healing don't make me more special than anyone else, nor does my ability to communicate them. They are simply the *why* behind my standing here with you, naked and yet clothed in Him, asking you to join me and God as I attempt to shake off those things that so easily beset me so that I can fly. I'm asking you to shake off yours as well.

Will you fly with me?

Course 1

The Starting Point: Who Am I?

Can't know where you're going until you know where you are.

In frenzied excitement he eats up the ground, he paws fiercely, rejoicing in his strength, then charges in the fray, afraid of nothing when the trumpet sounds.

SECRETARIAT

If thou knewest the gift of God, and who it is that saith to thee, Give me to drink; thou wouldest have asked of him, and he would have given thee living water.

JOHN 4:10

Thirsty. Parched. Drought of all droughts.

I am the woman at the well, the realization flooded over me. *And I don't want to be her anymore.* This admission was for me the birthplace of discovery, acceptance, and life.

You see, although I had come to Jesus and been beautifully forgiven and accepted and cleansed, I had not faithfully waited on Jesus or for my heavenly Father to lead me to His choice of a man for my life. Quite the contrary. I had grown weary in waiting. I had grown weary in well-doing. But I had grown even *more* weary in *not* well doing (see Gal. 6:9). I had played the harlot (ahem, spiritually speaking; see Hos. 2:5), and it had not served me at all. During those years I made many agreements not for God's glory but for mine, and worse, for Satan's.

At a certain point I experienced a painful breakup of worldly proportions, leaving my nerves shot, my heart broken, my weight diminished, in flooding me with confusion and epic shame. I was dying of thirst, and I knew it.

I needed to return to Jesus, my true Love, and find out who I was. Again.

I began with worship. I started singing a certain portion of the Psalms every morning. No measure or time, just raw emotion and conviction. This was my time of fellowship with God; I had nothing left to offer. I had defiled His temple, my body, and given my heart, once again, to a man who wasn't *mine*, but His Spirit in me prevailed, and we began our journey. I stumbled upon the story of the woman at the well in John 4, and I thought to myself, *Now here's a woman I can relate to.* What did Jesus have to say to her? How did He handle her heart and the lies that masked her adulterous choices?

In John 4:10 the Lord spoke to her about living water, and I embarked on a path of searching out "living water" throughout Scripture. My journey led me to promises about joy and to wells of salvation pouring water on our dry ground (see Isa. 44:3). To the promise of His Spirit being upon our seed and His blessing upon our offspring (see Ps. 69:36). And to the sad story about how we have forsaken Him, the fountain of living waters, and hewn for ourselves cisterns, broken cisterns, that can hold no water (see Jer. 2:13).

I found too that "in that day there shall be a fountain opened to the house of David and to the inhabitants of Jerusalem for sin and for uncleanness" (Zech. 13:1). "That day" has come, and it is still here.

My response?

In my famine and drought, I said, "Here I am, Lord. Here I am."

I started asking questions: how did I keep ending up at the base of the same mountains in my life? What did I need to break through to the land of abundance of peace, joy, and righteousness? What was I missing in my life that religion was not fulfilling? My heart started asking the questions, and the Lord answered by showing me things about myself, about Him, about life that would make all the difference and lead me to a whole life.

Knowing Ourselves—Knowing Him

Jesus told our girl that if she but "knew" with whom she was conversing and asked Him for living water, she would never thirst again. His call to me is no different. Neither is His call to you. As we set out on the journey to find out who we are, we have to find out who Jesus is first. We have to set our will daily and purpose in our heart to agree with our Dad so that we can *know* Jesus as much as possible on this side of eternity.

Why? Because Jesus is the embodiment of God's love, literally—and we are birthed in God. Love is our identity, and not as the ever-changing adjective that this word is assigned by culture. Love is not subjective. It's vast and glorious and just. It's righteous, peaceful, and filled with joy. It's who He is, and it's who we are.

To know someone in the biblical sense is to be about as intimate as one can be (see Gen. 4:1). I don't think it's a coincidence that Jesus used the term "know" with a woman who had been with several men she had called husband and who was, apparently, living that lie once again when she crossed paths with Him at the well (see John 4:10).

When we *know* someone, then *something* (sometimes physically but always spiritually) is conceived and subsequently birthed—unless it is aborted or miscarried (I've had both happen in the spiritual sense). Some relationships and life decisions I wish I had aborted *before* "knowing" them.

First Peter 3:7 tells husbands to dwell with their wives "according to *knowledge*." That entails getting to know her whims, her dreams, her likes and dislikes, what makes her feel safe. It's knowing *her* intimately, on the deepest of levels. Why? So that he can serve her wholly in love.

It may be time for us to ask ourselves, as longing single women, whether or not we actually know Jesus—and who we are in relation to Him. He's asking for the consideration, because He deserves it, and so do we. He deserves His inheritance, and we deserve life and more abundantly, because He died to give it to us. We deserve to live in the fullness of His purpose for us, because we were created for greatness in the form of righteousness, peace, and joy—otherwise known as salvation.

How do we do this? How do we *know* Jesus? Simple: by studying *Him*—in other words, His Word—and by walking through life with Him. He tells us in Matthew 11:29 that we are to do so. "Take my yoke upon you, and learn of me [study me]; for I am meek and lowly in heart: and ye shall find rest unto your souls." Hydration 101.

You may be completely parched and starving, or you may be saturated and stuffed in your love relationship with the Lord. Either way, I hope you glean from the meal of this book either a refreshing morsel of revelatory hope in your distress or a renewed resolve to continue on in the holiness that you are already pursuing.

Maybe you're one of the countless Christians who believe and nourish the lie that we are not holy and never will be, that somehow Jesus is the only holy being, and we can't measure up. Well, our Father thinks differently. And Jesus Christ tells us so. This is no-excuses territory. Open your mind to His. Open your ears to hear and your heart to receive. Contrary to the heresy that some preach today (see 1 Tim. 4:1), God's Spirit is *not* dead. He still speaks to us daily with fresh bread and living waters every second that we "look up" (see John 16:13; Luke 21:28)! (I remember being at a place in my faith at which I actually believed that God had said all that He was going to say to me, ever, just because I had read the Bible and felt that I knew what was in it. A *horrible*, stagnant place to be.)

So who are we?

Well, as Jesus told the woman at the well, to find that out we need to ask first, *whose* are we? We are betrothed, quite literally, to "God's gift to mankind" (see John 3:16; 4:10). When we put it that way for us girls who are generally attracted to the best, that's pretty cool! We are Christ's bride-to-be. And that makes Jesus our spiritual Fiancé.

To find out who *we* are, we have to put on "the mind of Christ" (1 Cor. 2:16). It is important for us to know what our Dad, the Father, thinks of us and how He feels about us, His creation. Yes, He has feelings for us, His daughters (see Ps. 117; Jer. 29:11; 31:3; John 3:16), but the only way we will ever know that is through His Son, His Love, our Fiancé, the Word. I have found that anything else is merely speculative humanism.

Before the Beginning

If we want to find out who we are, we need to start at the beginning.

I mean, we may be a mom, a daughter, a sister, a friend, a writer, a singer, an artist, an athlete, a bride-to-be, a worrier, a student, a product of our past, a thinker, an overly emotional sinning saint—but none of these are our real identity. So who are we? Like, really, *who* am I? Who are *you*? Why were we created?

Some of titles above are offices entrusted to us, but they do not serve us or others when they become our fundamental identity. On the contrary, they become taskmasters that rob us of the joy and satisfaction that we glean from partaking of them with excellence when we *first* know whose we are and then who we are.

It's my ministerial observation that many of us in Christianity begin the self-discovery process at the garden, at the fall, and we camp there. We wear labels—sinner, failure, broken, helpless—that bind us to an identity birthed in that fateful decision of Adam. We live a mediocre life steeped in excuses of the past—a past that has been paid for. We agree with the adage that we will never be perfect, according to the English language definition, and we skip through life with a limp.

But *God* tells us differently. He says that you and I are "fearfully and wonderfully" created beings (Ps. 139:14). We are simply mah-velous, dah-ling!

Let's stop right here and look those terms up.

"Fearfully" comes from a Hebrew word that means "to fear; morally to revere; causatively to frighten."[1]

Stop. This begs a question: since God has "not given us the spirit of fear" (2 Tim. 1:7), then in creating us "fearfully," who exactly does God intend to be afraid as a result of our being created? Who's supposed to do all the fearing and reverencing? Hmm. I have a good guess. Our *enemy*.

See, God said, "Let *us* make man in *our* image" (Gen. 1:26). This clarifies what Jesus meant when He said that we are equals with Him in friendship and kinship through our new birth (see John 15:15). Now don't get this twisted. I'm not saying that we're in the position of God. *He's* the Savior in all this, the Redeemer, the Lord; not us. But He called you and me *friends*. Joint heirs with Him (see Rom. 8:17). *That's major, ladies*!

On to the second and third characteristics of our identity.

"Wonderfully" means "to distinguish . . . put a difference, show marvelous, separate, set apart, sever, make wonderfully."[2] "Marvelous" means "to separate, that is, distinguish" or "great, difficult, wonderful," to "accomplish . . . hard, hidden, things too high . . . marvelous . . . miracles, perform, separate, make singular . . . wonderful . . . wondrous."[3]

I am a miracle. And so are you. A marvelously, wonderfully created being. You are an individual masterpiece. Does your soul know right well who and whose you are? To know this on the soul level means taking the time to discover things about ourselves. Oftentimes it includes venturing into new territories that can cause us discomfort, alienation, and uncertainty. But this is the place of formation with the potter and His clay. Going there requires courage and obedience, but it's worth it, because when we do, we will not have to rely upon exterior forces to tell us who and what we are. This is truly the place of communion between a Father and His daughters and a Fiancé and His beloved.

It's been my experience that life and the beauty of discovering ourselves really begins with accepting Jesus Christ as Savior at our new spiritual birth. The world has never taught me anything about myself. It has only projected itself onto me and saddled me with an identity not unique to me but instead to its own ways, ideals, and concepts, which are limited. That's a linear way of thinking and in direct contrast to the passionate freedom that my Father offers through Christ.

Through the eyes of our Fiancé, we are offered an unadulterated, unobstructed view of ourselves, free of worldly boundaries birthed in manmade ideologies, experiences, and concepts of lower-level living conjured in vain imagination. The truth is, we are built and established on precepts and endless love (truth) that know no bounds and are contrary to anything survival driven. All this provided by an intimate, passionate, caring, adoring God who wants us to know ourselves through first knowing Him.

Fragmented Theology, Fragmented Believers

You may have noticed "make singular" in the definition of the word "marvelous." It jumped off the page at me! We Christians tend to be a fragmented bunch. It's as if we live in many virtual realities, wearing multiple masks associated with our offices in life and never coming to a fundamental conclusion of who and what we are at our core. Therefore, we never rise above the fray, the matrix, the domain of beast, or our flesh, which is lower, satanic living in the order of creation (see Gal. 5:17–21).

A lot of us Christians are what I call amazing spiritual mixologists. In our efforts to figure out who we are, we tend to mix a little o' the world's ideas and a little o' the enemy's ideas and expect something other than a half-baked batch of weak faith. I've learned the hard (horoscope-reading) way that this kind of double-mindedness and pseudo-spirituality does not serve anything but the enemy's kingdom (James 1:8). It's time we choose God's way if we want a different result. Are we children of the finite zodiac or the infinite Creator of it? Are our lives subjected to moon cycles or to God's limitless plans and His ever-seeing eye and heart?

Many of us rest in the conclusion that because God is sovereign, somehow He is the only One capable of blessing us in life. But as we can see with Jesus' own temptation, Satan too is capable of serving up a plate of glitter and gold, and if we don't know our Fiancé's voice and promises, it's easy to take the devil up on his offers based on feelings and an ideology that says, "God allowed this, so it must be another learning experience."

I would submit to you that as a loving parent, I would not allow my daughter to play in traffic to teach her something. Living on this level of ignorance keeps us living as perpetual victims of an enemy that many of us deem as ourselves or others, but the result of this is that while we look and smell great, we are inwardly decaying. We not only need the truth, and now, we need to move in with *Him* and vacate the apartments of stinkin' thinkin', complacency, and bad choices based on a sin nature that many of us don't know that we can overcome.

Sadly, I've found through doing ministry with women that even in our Christianity, many of us don't really know whose, who, and what we are. Subsequently, we have no *living* understanding that we are a part of (as in birthed of, of blood relation with) something (and Someone) that matters. Someone who supersedes denominations and occupations. We hear these things, we say them, but in many cases, our lives are proof that we really don't believe and *know* them.

We can look around and see that our world is not in favor of order in a spiritual or physical sense. Consequently, we Christians live as orphaned beggars, adopting and adapting to the world's ways while claiming victory. God has given us so much more.

We are spiritual, physical, emotional, electrical, psychological, sexual, chemical, and genetically created beings.[4] It is often said that we can become so spiritually minded that we are of no earthly good—and I completely agree. Instead of nurturing and cultivating ourselves as entire beings from God's perspective, we sit atop our clouds of religious mantras that we call faith, peering down at the world while not looking much different from everyone else. Sigh.

Yes, our spirit man is the beginning of all abundant life and communication, but to dismiss the other parts of our created selves is to scoff at a perfect Creator who took *all* our humanity into consideration when He crafted us. He never meant for us to deny one part of ourselves to service another (with the exception of our flesh—the being of sin that serves the lower nature; see Rom. 7:17; Gal. 5:17).

When we first pursue, know, believe, and practice living from our authentic self as God proscribes through His Word, only then will we truly be able to serve Him, ourselves, and others. Only then, as women, will we see ourselves as secure, worthy, and beautiful. Our identity will become more evident and tangible as opposed to waiting for, as my former pastor likes to say, the banjo and white robe in the heavenlies. Heaven isn't just a destination; it's a daily existence.

We were created simply for *His* pleasure (see Rev. 4:11), not to do back flips in religion or jump from one square to the next to see if we got things right. We were created for intimacy with Him as we walk through this life.

Yet we live as if we are a fraction of Jesus and not in the abundant life He intends for us. I am curiously inclined to believe that They (the Godhead) never intended for us to be fragmented, scattered beings (see Gen. 1:26). We are whole as our Father is whole, because we are His offspring (see Matt. 5:48). Quite literally. Nothing missing. They put us here knowing that those vomited created beings (fallen angels) were not far from us, and They trusted us with all creation in spite of it (see Rev. 12:9). I see this as the ultimate act of trust and hope. His provision in the cross proves it (see 1 Pet. 1:20).

Did we blow it? Yes. *But God.* (I use the term "But God" often in our meal, because when we include God in our lives, we can not only count on reparation but will *see* it in a big way (see Exod. 20:6). While we have been regenerated in spirit, which is a work of the Holy Spirit (our Father's power), it appears that we have some distance to go in the renewing of our minds and the turning of our hearts in this thing called sanctification and moving from glory to glory (see 2 Cor. 3:18). It requires a rewiring of our magnificent brains that have been trained in the law of sin (see Rom. 7:5–6) to the point that I call "being disfigurement."

We are spiritually stunted. Reminds me of a guy I met recently who was stuck. Stuck in his youth, which led him to act, think, and feel as if he was still in college. The sad part is, although he was a great guy and tons of fun, he was nearly instantaneously ousted from my dating roster because I'm not in college any longer, and his concept of life abundant and mine made us unequally yoked. He didn't know who he was as a man, so he existed as a boy.

For too many of us, our lives are proof that we've got some growing up to do spiritually. As women, we gossip, fear, covet, shack, suspect, curse, lie, cheat, compete, steal, neglect, worry, compare, strive, and on and on, just as the world does. This isn't an accusation based in hopelessness; it's an observation worthy of repeal. We can't change what we won't face. Have you asked your Creator what He takes pleasure in regarding you? You may be surprised and comforted and filled with new hope and dreams.

It's time, ladies. We are called to more. Because we *are* more.

Just a Girl

Now before you get your lacies in a bunch, read on.

People at a church I attended for years regularly used the statement "You're just a girl." On some level it irked me—that level that says, "Ha! Are you kidding me?! *Just* a girl? Do you know what I've done as *just* a girl to work this thing called life? The long nights for years in the hospital with my sick child; retrieving firewood in winter months to keep us warm; running two companies; raising a child, successfully, alone; all while managing our home? Um, what do you *mean, just a girl*?!" It's that ferocious self that rises to convince me that somehow I've done good, on my own, without the covering of our Fiancé.

But during those moments when my Iron Woman cape is all worn out, I realize the absolutely beautiful mercy and call to rest in that one statement. While in Christ we aren't male or female (see Gal. 3:28), men and women are, in fact, designed differently from one another, and we women need our heavenly Family (the Godhead), not culture, to show us the delicacies of who we are and the role we've been placed here to fill. We are indeed girls. And that is a wonderful thing.

"Delicate" is not a four-letter word, just FYI. While women are, in fact, capable of leading people and making management decisions (see Judg. 4), whether in the pantry, battlefield, or boardroom, we are His *girls* in creation, and that assignment carries with it a place in the order of creation different from that of a man. It's a beautiful and responsible thing to be a girl, no matter what lies have been exalted above the throne of truth (see Isa. 14:13). There is covering for us, and rest.

When we pursue our true identity in the order of creation, we effortlessly beam with the beauty, poise, grace, and confidence that we all seek to exude. An instant facelift! (I like that—"Righteousness, the Instant Facelift." Ha.)

If we really knew and appropriated the truth of who and whose we are, the world's images of beauty would be of ill effect on us. And the world would see it and, at the very least, inquire.

While we schlep the loads of the world on our female frames girded in pride, insecurity, and the wearing of masks (diseases common to women are evidence of this), may we give ourselves permission and set our wills to apply this time to gather at His feet, cast everything upon Him because He tells us to, and receive from Him. Can we receive our rest, identity, instruction, purpose, worth, salvation, peace, joy, and sanity? Can we live our very best life now, even if we're still ordering for one? Can we allow our God-given beauty to rise up from the ashes of life, trusting that we are enough and not listening to the accusation that we are somehow too much? Praise be to God. Glory!

Cleansing Your Palate

Now's the time for you to step back and allow the course you've just partaken of to settle. Together with your sisters with whom you're sharing this meal, talk through the questions below, and look up the Scriptures listed.

You've read a bit of my story—now consider yours. Do you know who you are? Do you know Jesus? Go to Him, as the woman at the well did, as I did, and begin to fill your heart with His living water. As you begin to know Him, or to know Him again, you will begin to find your true self—and life abundant.

I encourage you to recognize where some of your theology may differ from the simple, beautiful, and honest truth of what God says about you. As you recognize discrepancies and long-held beliefs and choices that have never served you or your generations, and never will, confess these to your Father, repent of them, renounce them—and get on with your new clean temple filled with His Spirit! You're worth it, and so is He.

Pray with your sisters, and be renewed. Remember—righteousness is an instant facelift.

* How would you describe your current emotional, spiritual, mental, and physical health?

* List any areas in your life in which you feel starved or parched.

* If you met Jesus along your path today, what would He say to you? In response to Him, what and who in your life would stay or go?

- Where are you right now in your relationship and journey with the Lord Jesus (your Fiancé), Father God, and the Holy Spirit?

- What do you think They (the Godhead) think of you?

- What do *you* think of you?

- Why were you created?

DIG A LITTLE DEEPER

Look up Psalm 139, Matthew 5:48, and Matthew 11:29, and share with your sisters or write down what each passage says about your identity and purpose.

Course 2

Drinking from the Wrong Wells

My people have committed two evils; they have forsaken me the fountain of living waters, and hewed them out cisterns, broken cisterns, that can hold no water.

JEREMIAH 2:13

Let's start with the obvious enticement that most of us single girls face—those awesome fellow dustbowls: men.

What is it about the arm of man (see Jer. 17:5) that leads us away from our fountain of living waters? What is the draw? I would venture to say that for every woman it is different. We are told in the Word that it is of our own lusts that we are drawn away and enticed (see James 1:14). When lust is conceived, it brings forth sin and, ultimately, death.

Now having a desire for a man is a perfectly *natural, God-given* desire. But in all honesty, as single ladies, it's hard to wait, and wait, and wait, feeling the years slip by as we watch our friends enjoy weddings, baby showers, new homes, the milestones of their kids . . . (You know, like when we go to those events with a bright smile, dressed all cute with our strappy heels and new clutch just in case some single Boaz is in attendance, all while that little naggy voice says, "Hmm, why did *she* get such a blessing?" "What's wrong with *me*?" "When will it be *my* turn?" or the best of the lying voices for us Christian girls, "She must be holier than me." That's my personal fave.) In our loneliness and frustration, it's easy to get ourselves tangled up in with guys we should *not* entertain, and if you're anything like me, we can eventually come to the end of our own wells where men are concerned. I personally have had it with married women telling me, albeit in love, that Jesus is my husband and that I should just be patient in the waiting—all while I'm successfully doing face plants in the waiting.

But I'm ready to receive manna, honey, and a new straight path (see Deut. 8:1–10; Isa. 42:16)! I need some fresh water, baby, and there's only one well we can get it from! Are you with me?

As for being drawn away, let's face it, sometimes we fall. A different arm, a different face, different promises, different gifts, different cologne, a different career, a different car. But the same sin with the same result: *nothing*. Alas, the cisterns we drink from prove to be only dust (as in human) like us (see Ps. 103:14). In turn, our hearts end up broken vessels, unable to hold any water. Over time, if we aren't careful, we begin to walk through life holding bitter conversations about men due to secret self-resentment concepts that we *think* no one else can see or hear. Oh, but they can.

Now I am *not* saying that we can't have a God-given appreciation for the awesomeness (and hotness) of God's other creatures called men—don't go zealot on me. I'm saying that we shouldn't use those creations and be used by them for purposes other than God's life.

As we partake of this meal with the Word (our Fiancé), He reminds us of the foolishness of putting our faith in the arm of man who cannot save—whether our own arm or someone else's.

Who Are You in Love With?

As single ladies, we, along with Christ, are the keepers of our hearts—not men. Men are not our cistern. That job is reserved for our Fiancé.

If Jesus said that *He* is the well of living waters (see John 4:10), shouldn't we be drinking from *Him*? If He is not the Rock we have hewn our cistern from, we are in trouble. We are dependent upon others' rocks or our own. Both miserable, fragile sustainers. We are but clay.

We are hewn from dirt. But *He* is the Rock of our salvation. Jesus. Our Fiancé. He is our tall glass of lemonade on a desperately hot Southern day. Living waters flow from Him and have since the beginning.

Jesus told the woman at the well that if she but *knew* the gift of God standing before her, she would ask for and be *quenched* with living water and never thirst again. Wow. That's pretty powerful.

I don't know about you, but the oases in my deserts just aren't cutting it anymore. Hello? I've dated enough men who think they are *the* gift to women (not in a godly way), and it's old news. I want, need, and am learning to appreciate, through fellowship with like-minded sisters, the living waters of my Fiancé.

In my quest to learn more about this being-in-love-with-Jesus business, when I got totally real, I realized that I was not sure that I'd ever been "in love" with Jesus. How about you? Relax. Take a deep breath and get honest about your own level of being in love.

Would you turn down a date with (insert man of your dreams) because Jesus was asking you to more prayer time after work? Would you forego that third adult bevie at girl's night out so you could be sober enough for Him to comfort you instead? For some of you, are you so in love with Jesus that you would stay in and snuggle with Him (the Word) over the weekend when you'd been invited by Mr. Hubba-Hubba on an all-expense-paid trip via private plane to a remote, romantic island with a yacht, fully staffed, waiting for you? "In love" with Jesus. Yep. Thought so.

Remember (if you read the story in John 4), our girl at the well was shackin,' and truth be told, many of us are too—if not literally, in the crevices of our hearts and imaginations on levels we can't conceive, much less admit (wave the white hanky and say amen, ladies). Don't confuse my honesty with condemnation. But we can't change what we won't admit, face, and actively turn from.

Now I believe, as many of you do, that Jesus is who God says He is and who He shows Himself to be through the Scriptures: the only begotten Son of God, who died for our sins, was resurrected by our Father, and is seated at the right hand of our Father. I am thankful for His sacrifice, and I have worshiped Him in song, in spirit and truth (see 4:24). But when the winds blow at the right moment and my feelings inch back onto the throne of my life, or when I follow the voice of comparison, fear, or accusation against God ("Poor me, I've just been left out of the good-man pool and should probably just plan on blue-hair-discount grocery days with my besties"), I begin to tread on dangerous ground. Well, let me call it what it really is: cheating-whoredom ground.

That's a tough and ugly term, but we need a clear, sober picture of what our wandering looks like to our Father and to the One who died and rose to save us—our Fiancé, Jesus. It's just ugly. Painfully ugly. Because They know that the all-expense-paid trip with Mr. Hot and that third beverage or the maxed-out credit cards leave us wanting and destitute and, more importantly, estranged from the life that They long to give us.

While We're Chatting about the Boyz . . .

In a time in which boys are being raised by mothers in epic numbers, I'd like to say, as an aside, that we need more men to raise up other men, and the church should be the place to begin. There are just some things a mama can't teach a boy when it comes to being a man.

Men were placed here to cover us from the beginning, and instead they blamed us when the whole thing literally went to hell in a hand basket (see Gen. 3:12). But I don't subscribe to man bashing—I don't believe in it. I avoid women who engage in it at all costs. That is a malignant spirit I can't afford to align with, and neither can you. (Now with as much drama as men have assisted me with, you *know* Jesus must be at work in my life, because I could host a man-roast of biblical proportions. But God.)

I actually think men have it pretty hard. They are undervalued while dressed for success, hoping that they have what it takes. Look no further than your prime-time television dummy dad, whom the entire family mocks and emasculates.

A part of each man, as buried as his hopes may be, still believes that he has what it takes; he wants to swoop in and save the day, because that's our Father's wiring for him. But because of the enemy and a degenerating society, we are rapidly watching the feminization of a gender that was not confused in the beginning, when God created him. It's not inherent in men to run away from responsibilities, honor, and accountability the way many do today. If we would speak to men according to the place God created them for—that of greatness—they would trip over themselves to live up to it.

This begins with those entrusted to rear them. It is a privilege to raise a child, whether a girl or a boy, and we should know with certainty that we are preparing that child to be a blessing or a curse to the world—a liability or an asset. As for us girls, well, we came from man: "The rib, which the LORD God had taken from man, made he a woman" (Gen. 2:22). Some of us need to ask why we hate what we were literally created from—someone so much a part of ourselves. We were created for their companionship.

We could go on and on about our role in men's lives, but this book is about us *apart* from a man, because we deserve to be whole, whether single or not, and the world deserves whole women. But I wasn't going to speak to you about wholeness as my single sisters and not bring our awesome counterparts into the conversation, even if briefly. I have witnessed men in ministry who have every kind of issue the enemy could throw at them and have seen their accompanying tears, regret, shame, and fear of never being accepted, and it has healed me in ways I can't count. It has birthed in me a real love for men and a recognition of the language they speak: respect.

As another aside, we girls could use a real lesson in the language of respect, not only as it regards men but also in dealing with each other. Are all the choices that men and women make worthy of respect? Of course not. But the love we should extend to one another as brothers and sisters hasn't changed, because it's birthed in a never-changing God. We can extend forgiveness, mercy, and grace and still keep our hearts intact.

Other Wells

Men aren't the only object of our pursuit of fulfillment. We hew our own cisterns from careers and pleasures and other pursuits as well. In this meal we are focusing mainly on men, because I am a widow—and because I like men! And, as I mentioned, I am the woman at the well. But I run into so many sisters who strive for a great many things, position being one of them. This causes a huge separation between them and the ones whose places they covet. It's divisive and satanic. The disciples did this too. Same devil, different era (see Luke 9:46–48; 22:24–27).

We drink from wells of entertainment too. As a songwriter and recording artist, I listen intently to words and to the intentions behind them. You may have noticed, as I have, how the words of songs can move everything from our feelings to our hormones. I can feel sexy, sassy, angry, happy, redeemed, hopeful, desperate, or domineering, all from a simple song. It is truly amazing what we agree with on an emotional and basic human level as we drive down the street or work it on a dance floor. If we follow those feelings and sing aloud to the words in complete agreement, no matter how innocent that seems, we are agreeing with those words, and they will affect us. No doubt about it. Music influences many things, scientifically and otherwise.

If artists only knew the power they hold in influencing decisions, feelings, and actions, they might be shocked in dismay or grieved. Now listen, I'm not some music Nazi, nor do I subscribe to censorship of any kind, but I'm speaking as a creator and as your fellow sister in Christ. The world is singing about S&M and day drinking, and we need to be aware of the influences we allow into our eyes and ears and, subsequently, into our minds and hearts. Why? Because what we listen to often diminishes the truth that Jesus really can fill all our crevices of wounding, hope, desire, sadness, and despair without our having to tie someone up (or vice versa) or stay high to get over someone.

Yes, I find myself humming these things too, and then I stop and listen, and the lyrics always point me to what I call the being of flesh. Pretty simple.

I found myself blowing it out one night to a well-known pop artist who wanted to be someone's only girl (in the world), and when I realized the power, anger, and retribution I was singing along with, I thought that I may as well have been in black leather chaps, with a whip, driving down the road. No kidding. I was incredibly mad, wanting someone to pay for all the mistakes I had made, angry with every less-than-stellar dude I had ever encountered. The conviction with which I sang startled me and, thankfully, led me to some quiet time with the Lord to search out that wound and allow Him to heal it.

Music isn't our only seducer from the entertainment world. When we butter our popcorn at a movie that features a well-dressed but too-skinny guy and that makes neckties and dog collars on bedposts look intoxicating, we need to ask ourselves, *what* are we subjecting ourselves to? Anything that requires humiliation or abuse is *not* of our Father's kingdom, no matter how cute the panties or how great the music that lures us into our own fantasies.

Yep. I don't know about you, but I can follow an emotional fantasy like nobody's business, and before I know it, I'm discontent, comparing, feeling a bit frisky, and accusing God of not fulfilling my every want, whim, or need. I'm definitely *not* feelin' the Jesus love, and then I'm back in goofy-decisionville. And, as we touched on, it doesn't have to be a guy that draws us away from our true cistern. It can mean a tub of ice cream or too many drinks with the girls or someone else's position at work or shopping till we drop or . . .

Guys are not the problem. The enemy, religion, self-ignorance, and willful choices in agreement with our flesh are. We look to pleasures and passions and position and the feelings that these bring to sustain desires that no man or pleasure could ever fulfill. But God.

Knowing and Being Known

I wonder how much of our drivenness to dig our own wells is caused by a deep desire to be known. When we take the time to draw from Jesus as our cistern and get to know Him, the man at the well, He actually shows us who we are. We become blessed with His insight to us regarding our personalities, gifts, and talents, and we can then use these gifts, free of comparison. We can run our race fully, because we are fully understood and thus free. We become ridiculously attractive to the entire world. A basic need of humans is to be understood, but the only way to achieve that is through knowing Him first.

When my daughter left for college, one of her biggest concerns was leaving the one person who *knows* her, who really gets her: Mommy. She and I have spent an inordinate amount of time together by American standards, due to my call and subsequent surrender to homeschool her when she was in the second grade. We also weathered many years of a chronic illness together, which placed me in the role of a caregiver and her in that of a patient. We *know* each other because we have spent countless hours communicating with each other about everything: politics, history, the weather, our favorite shows, guys, friends, , themes of life, struggles, life, death, and living the Word. With perfection? No. But in honest acceptance and trust of each other and, more importantly, of the One caring for us.

She has learned in our time apart that the One who knows her best isn't me, her mother, but her heavenly Father, who carefully knitted her together, and her Fiancé, who walks through life with her. In my absence and with 2,200 miles of distance from me, she has had to call on His name more than once to ask for and receive comfort, clarity, and reminding.

We are no different. Jesus is our answer.

So how do we put down our cultural creature comforts and drink from the Rock that provides the wells of living waters? It's pretty simple: we have to understand who Jesus is and who He is not.

Jesus is *not* our Father. Our Father is our Father (see John 14:6–7). Jesus came as our servant. He is the greatest among us, and He still serves us today. And Jesus is *not* our husband; as we mentioned earlier, He is our Fiancé (see Matt. 25:10).

Jesus is our friend (see John 15:15). He is our Redeemer (see Isa. 44:24), our brother (see Rom. 8:29), our defense attorney (see 1 John 2:1). He is the way, the truth, the life (see John 14:6). He is the Word (see 1:1–5). He will be our judge, not Father God (see Rom. 14:10; 2 Cor. 5:10; 2 Tim. 4:1; 1 Pet. 4:5). Jesus is what every girl and woman on the planet wants: the lover of our souls (see Ps. 116).

As we start spending time with Jesus and begin to understand who He is to us and for us, hopefully our hearts will be ignited to *know* more about Him, this mysterious man of our faith. I like the word "mysterious," because it points to intimacy, to something to be unveiled. I would venture to say that most of us see men as one-dimensional, lacking in depth—that's how society sells them to us. But Jesus is part of a triune whole. He's nothing short of one revealed mystery after another. We, as His beloved bride-to-be, are to discover Him and let Him pursue us, both one on one and collectively.

As we draw near to Jesus to know Him and be known by Him, many of us stop at the "I believe! See ya when I die!" but for us to know anything about the character, heart, mind, and vision of the One we are spending eternity with, thus to know ourselves, we must show up at the well in faith and transparency. I *almost* said in surrender, but the truth is, many of us sleep with our fists clinched and one eye open, yes, even toward Him. Some of us aren't ready to surrender. That proverbial white flag is neatly tucked under the pillow in the bed we share either with a man who isn't ours or with our fantasies of a life to come.

When we come to Him in fellowship, which we do through and *with* His Word, the Bible, He nourishes, covers, cares for, serves, instructs, and corrects us (see Ps. 91; 2 Tim. 3:16). He redeems us not only from eternal death but from death in the now (see John 10:10; 17:3)—the death of our minds, our spirits, our bodies. He redeems us from wrong thinking and wrong feeling and, therefore, from wrong choices and poor health. He empowers us to live courageously and to make right, healthy choices in peace, not false religion that drives us to perform.

Jesus redeems us from generational curses that run in genetic coding through our DNA (see Ps. 103:3). He gives us the gift of appropriating what He gave for us: His life. His body and His blood.

Jesus gave all. For us. We start here.

He chose us first; we did not choose Him first. He said so. *They* chose us first (see John 15:16). And Their hope for us begins and ends in God's only begotten Son, Jesus the Christ, slain from the foundation of the world (John 3:16; Rev. 13:8).

Cleansing Your Palate

- Whom do you trust?
  (Include yourself, if you make the cut.)

- What do you imagine that God and Jesus think of your
  personal life? Of the desires of your heart?

- How do you handle revealed sin in your life?

- From what are you drinking and feeding?

- What/who comforts you?

- Do you feel known? If so, by whom?

DIG A LITTLE DEEPER

Look up Jeremiah 17:5, John 4:10, and John 15:15,
and share with your sisters or write down what each
passage says about the results of drinking from the
wrong well and of drinking from the right well.

Course 3

Cycles of Whoredom

My people are destroyed for lack of knowledge: because thou hast rejected knowledge, I will also reject thee, that thou shalt be no priest to me: seeing thou hast forgotten the law of thy God, I will also forget thy children.

HOSEA 4:6

As I sat down to prepare this course of our meal, Hosea 4:6 had me sorrowfully shaking in my shoes over God's loving chastisement regarding a few things in my life. I spent some time in James too:

> Cleanse your hands, ye sinners: and purify your hearts, ye double minded. Be afflicted and mourn, and weep: let your laughter be turned to mourning and your joy to heaviness. Humble yourselves in the sight of the Lord, and he shall lift you up. (James 4:8–10)

My personal conversation with the Lord after reading these Scriptures went something like this: "How is it, Lord, that knowing all the above, I still return to whoredom? Because I have rejected knowledge, will You now reject me? Who could speak against it if You did? It is not Your fault that I have gone astray, Dad."

"Lack of knowledge has taken you into captivity," He replied. "I will bring and am bringing you out through My mercy and grace."

Getting sober (proverbially speaking) can be rough (see 1 Pet. 5:8). The things we whore after have their teeth sunk deeply into us. (The term "whoredom," by the way, is not gender specific—it points to a heart and head condition and applies to all of us—men and women—the same. Samey-samey.) No matter who we are, it's not easy to quit our patterns of sinning and sorrowing and sinning again.

Why is that?

I'm not here to debate your theological principles, but I want to shed some light on a few things that His church, His bride-to-be, often tends to overlook as we stare into the eyes of grace while carrying on in our sin.

Time to Get Serious

Hosea tells us that a lack of knowledge leads to destruction (see Hos. 4:6; Jon. 2:8). This is our problem. We fail to inform ourselves regarding God's truth, and in that state, we are open to captivity—and our enemy has no mercy.

Speaking of our enemy, many of us think that we ourselves, or other people, are the enemy. On the contrary, Ephesians 6:12 tells us exactly who and what our enemy is, and, astoundingly enough, *we* aren't listed. How can we do battle when we don't know who our enemy is?

Ephesians 6 goes on to tell us exactly how to suit up for this battle to ensure our success. But for many of us, this is just another list of do's and would never make it past the fashion police of today's spiritual standards for what's hot and what's not. (Some of our own pastors tell us that the Bible is irrelevant in today's world, so it's no wonder that we are standing on the field of life buck naked shouting victory! Crazy.)

The point is, due to our ignorance of God's Word and our efforts to do battle against sin in our birthday suits (ahem), whether willfully or otherwise, we end up in captivity—without peace, joy, or fellowship. We become literally imprisoned by our besetting sins. Our lack of knowledge, understanding, and wisdom leaves us vulnerable prey.

So what does the Word, our Fiancé, have to say to us on the issue of sin?

Some pretty succinct and sobering things, actually: "Remember therefore from whence thou art fallen, and repent, and do the first works; or else I will come unto thee quickly, and will remove thy candlestick out of his place" (Rev. 2:4–5). In other words, *repent* and *return* or your relationship with Him will face grave consequences.

If you fall into this category of having left your first love, that is, *Him*, I suggest taking heed, in spite of the warm fuzzies that some of our false shepherds give us. We are responsible for our sanctification and for our choice to fellowship and agree with sinful things. While God is faithful to finish the good work He began in us, our yes or no to Him matters. Our choices have consequences; obedience is greater than sacrifice. We won't be able to drag our occluded pastors with us to the judgment seat of Christ. (Not to worry, pastors will be held accountable too. Spiritual leaders are held to a standard that most of us would not want on a good day. In spite of how some of them live now, they will face a day of accounting for what they fed to our Father's flocks. And so will I for this meal I'm offering.)

At times it may seem that we are getting away with things as we skip down God Knows My Heart Lane, but by His mercy, God's Spirit convicts us and summons us to turn. The greasy-grace slope is no match for our perfect God. He is indeed "faithful and just" to forgive us our sins and cleanse us from all unrighteousness when we confess our sin to Him (1 John 1:9), but instead of using that truth as a free-willy license to keep on with the keep on, we need to get real about who and whose we are. *Very* real (see Rom. 6:1–23). Remember, we are His bride-to-be, and He is our Fiancé.

The *truth* is, grace does not abound so that sin may abound more (see Rom. 6:1–2). Sin still separates us from God and brings death, on multiple levels. First Corinthians 6:9–10 and Galatians 5:21 tell us exactly who is *not* going to inherit the kingdom: people who *practice* the sins these passages list. If you are a practicing sinning saint and believe that your behavior is okay because "God understands" and all your sins, present, past, and future, are paid for, it's time to seriously reconsider your path. Repentance is the only way out (Lam. 3:40; 2 Tim. 2:25).

This teaching is hard for me to write. My own tears are flowing, tears of shame and guilt (see Gen. 3:7). I know these tears are not from my Father but because of agreements I made with the enemy that took me captive. Because of them I get to feel his accusatory lies and his kingdom railing against me—that is, until I call upon my Fiancé, the Word, to rescue me in my repentance.

I've given in to the voices of comparison and accusation (see Gen. 3:1) that tell me God could not care less about my personal life or the desires of my heart. I have coveted men, and, at times, I have greatly disliked them. I have acted as their counselor, comforter, and great spiritual redeemer (little r), and I have unsuccessfully missionary dated (more on that in a later course). (Lord help us! If it were up to us women to get men into heaven, the kingdom would be empty.)

I've been content (see 1 Tim. 6:6), I've been discontent. I've read books, I've burned books. I've sought counsel and taken advice (see Prov. 11:14), I've said, "Forget counsel," and gone my own way. I've forsaken my child (see Ps. 27:10), I've forsaken myself (see 1 John 3:20), and I have even taken my heart back from the One I had given it to, my Savior and faithful Fiancé, per His sweet request (see John 15:16).

Like a child completely busted and feeling the grief of my parents, I know that I have grieved my Father's Spirit. I sit in silence and type, not daring to deny or defend my past choices. How can I—I'm the chick at the well, remember? Job comes to mind (see Job 42:6). So does David (see Ps. 51:4). I could blame my actions on the enemy of my soul (honestly, he and my agreements with him, along with the agreements of my ancestors in the way of generational rebellion against God's Word, played a large part in my downfall). But as with deceptive pastors, Satan will not be present with me at my day of judgment (see 1 Cor. 3:13), nor will any of the dustbowls who have tried to drag me away from my birthright. We will each stand alone before our Fiancé and give account. I want to hear, "Job well done, good and *faithful* servant."

So I'm asking God to help me in the process of overcoming my mess by weeding my heart of my whoredom and setting me free from guilt, shame, apathy, arrogance, fear, and religion (among other things; see Ps. 51:2) so that I can actually feel the excitement of looking into my Fiancé's eyes and hearing, "Welcome, my beloved, come and dine with Us" (Rev. 3:20). (Goats are cute, but I *don't* want to spend my eternity with *them*—check 'em out in Matthew 25:31–46. I've dated enough of them here. Just sayin'.)

Despite the sorrow involved in repentance, keep this good news in mind: when *one* sinner repents, all heaven rejoices (see Luke 15:7)! And the gates of hell shall not prevail against the Rock of heaven (Matt. 16:18)—our cistern. (So remember to show up for your own party! I imagine a monster party in the heavenlies like TV's George Jefferson-shuffle kind of party. Ha. More on celebrating in a later course of this meal.)

Holy Vessels

I find that *many* of my sisters in the body of Christ today flagrantly agree with the defiling of their bodies. It's almost a single's rite of passage. And we don't hear much these days about hell and damnation regarding sex in its unlawful context, because many churches simply don't discuss the issue for fear of not being relevant. Well, our bodies are always relevant to our Father, because the Holy Spirit dwells in them. Our bodies are His temple.

What exactly does it mean to defile something? It means to spoil, desecrate, debase, impair, profane, or degrade it. Defilement begins in our hearts and minds. We are clean, and we are the vessels of the Lord. The Lord used to dwell in a vessel made with hands (the Ark of the Covenant). Look in the mirror: you are now the vessel of the Holy Spirit. So what are you sharing *His* vessel with?

When, after being washed by the Lord, we return to our proverbial vomit and wallow in the mud (see 2 Pet. 2:22), imagine what happens in the heavenlies: our Father is inundated day and night with the accuser condemning you and me to our Dad. Day and night. Imagine a six-year-old in a parent's face day and night, 24/7, telling what the four-year-old did. *That* is what our Dad gets to hear daily. And guess who hears it first? Our Fiancé.

Can you imagine the absolute delight that Satan takes in luring us into beds where we don't belong and then hitting the play button on the great slide show of our lives for our Fiancé to see? Yuck. It's not as if our Fiancé doesn't know what we are up to and when and with whom, but the enemy reminding Him of our failings is the equivalent of having the woman who stole your man show up with pictures day and night to remind you of who he is with now after you gave everything (but your actual life) to him. Uh, yeah. Very yuck.

Now listen, again, this is *not* to bring condemnation. I'm fighting every condemning demon from hell mixed with honest, godly remorse as I type this (see 2 Cor. 7:10), but I gotta tell ya, defiling our vessel, the temple of the Holy Spirit, is no joke. We need to be aware of what fools us, who lures us, what sends our hormones into orbit, what gives us the tinglies, what and who leads us astray to vain imaginations: fantasy movies, our own reels, songs, novels, others' comments and opinions, not-so-happy hour with the girls, comparison, entitlement, jealousy, bitterness, self-pity, coveting, brokenness, hope deferred, wantonness, *fear*. Phew. Yes, all these can cause defilement of our vessel, because they aren't of our Father.

Sexual sin carries with it greater issues than these, because as Paul states, it's against *our* body. When we engage in it, we sin against ourselves as well as our Father and Fiancé. We usher in disorder, because with fornication and adultery there is no covenant, no real skin in the game (horrible analogy, I know, but one worth using here).

We are Jesus' bride-to-be, sealed for Him by the Holy Spirit. Why would we want to pollute our vessels that belong to Him?

Lusty Lust

So why *do* we return to our vomit and go down paths that we know for sure will *not* lead to life and that more abundantly? Well, it's certainly not because our faithful Father tempts us with evil. Our Love tells us so in James 1:13. This does away with the notion that somehow God brought someone else's husband into our path to see if we could handle it or that our loving Father somehow hooked us up with that abusive guy because He just knew that we were the special daughter to change him. Um, yeah. Not so much. Come *on*, ladies!

The enemy tells *all* of us these lies on some level or another, and we repeat them to each other over coffee or cocktails and, worse, believe them, right into the pit.

So what is it exactly that leads us into our individual sins? As we covered in the last course of this meal, according to our Fiancé, it's because every man or woman is tempted when we are drawn away of our *own lust* and enticed. He also goes on to tell us exactly what transpires when lust is *conceived*. It brings forth sin, and sin, when it is finished, brings forth *death* (see James 1:14–15).

Now most of us see the word "lust" and instantly think of something sexual. *Stop.* Lust, according to our Fiancé, is setting our heart upon something,[1] usually something forbidden. It's being driven by the lower bestial nature.[2] Lust is an inordinate setting of our eyes and heart on something birthed in none other than our flesh. It is not living according to our highest self (righteousness).

Basically, lust means to *take*. The enemy knows this and fans the flames of our natural, God-given desires in the hopes that we will *take* for ourselves something that God has already promised that *He* would supply within the proper order, motivation of our heart, and time (see Ps. 37:4; Matt 6:33).

Let's look at a few examples of how being lusty creeps up on us: Daydreaming of hooking up with someone we're not married to or being the wife of a man who already has one is an obvious lust issue. So is hoping that the woman who's up for a promotion is discredited so that we get it. Or hoping that our ex's new girl somehow steps in front of a bus in her new Louboutins after a day of fun with the man we used to call ours. But there are less obvious ones, such as neglecting our family and friends to earn that deserved spot on the church board because it will show all those naysayers and say something to us about our worth. Or neglecting ourselves by not eating properly in order to attain that ideal body that we think someone will want one day. Dreading life, complaining, and making comparisons can also make lust lists.

Basically, anything contrary to our Father's way of thinking, feeling, and behaving can land on the lust list. They become addictions. And what are addictions but fillers for those places that we won't let Him fill with His love. We were designed for love. Created for it. When *His* is missing, we seek it out through other mediums, and there's really no end to how that manifests.

But every facet and manifestation of lust, whether big or small, plays a role in charting a course toward separation from God, self, and others—in other words, death.

Make Your List, Check It Twice

If we want to successfully change our behavior and keep our vessels *clean*, we must first see and confess the condition of our heart and become obedient to our God-proscribed life. Healing begins here, and healthy choices can then emerge.

Instead of longingly fantasizing and lusting after that man we want, the kind of guy "everyone else" has, we have the right to be in intimate, real, honest, fellowship with the *only* One who knows us intimately. We need to ask our Fiancé the serious questions: "Who am I?" "What is *Your* dream and hope for my life?" (see Prov. 3:6). "How special am I to *You*?" (Remember, as we saw earlier, to understand His answers or even to receive anything that He may reveal in answer to our questions, we must ask Him first who *He* is. It is in knowing *Him* that we get the real picture of who *we* are.)

We need to ask God the tough questions too: "What are my personal and generational lusts that drag me away into enticement and inevitably back into captivity?" (see James 1:15). Yes, as yuck and scary as it may feel, this is the moment in our meal for you to ask in prayer for the revelation (not an accusation or a condemnation) of what is in your own heart that keeps you creeping back to bondageville. Our Father will be faithful to show you by His Spirit. Why? *Because He loves you.*

Here's a newsflash: with or without a man, our lusts are with us, and they are nasty. I've asked Dad for an exhaustive list of mine, and let me tell you, in His mercy He gave me a small but crucial list to begin with. It was eye-opening. (Yeah. Had to look up the definition of some of mine. My flesh stinks.)

He will be faithful to show you (not kill you with the truth of) the things that lure you and ensnare you. He will also give you the knowledge to make an educated decision and the free will (that He paid for) to choose sanctification out of respect and gratitude for your salvation and for the One who provided it. He will be faithful to give you the opportunity to choose *life* (see Deut. 30:19; Rom. 6:12).

You can keep your list to yourself or share it with a friend or with your group. I'm not saying that you should let it all hang out. I *am* encouraging you to find a safe soul (or souls) to share things with, if you are so led, and get this stuff off your heart. If you choose to share your list, you will be amazed at how common to humanity your lust list is. Nothing uncommon to man has befallen us (see 1 Cor. 10:13). Remember, if we confess our faults to one another, we are healed (see James 5:16).

I love that James 5:16 goes on to say that we should "pray one for another" and that the "prayer of a righteous man availeth much." Reminds me too that one can put one thousand to flight and two, ten thousand (see Deut. 32:30). I like those odds. It's worth the risk of sharing your list with a safe group or person so that you (and they) can be set free! In sharing with others, we aren't trusting in man, we are living our faith by relying on His Word to do what it set out to do—and that always involves *freedom*. Woot! I'm excited just typing this!

So get out a sheet of paper and ask away regarding your lust list.

But beware of this: as the Lord shows you wounding, open doors in your life to sin habits, and familial and generational lusts in your heart, be vigilant to watch for those feelings of condemnation, confusion, and accusation, *none* of which represent our Father's character or heart. Ever.

The enemy whispers blame and accusation to us on spiritual level, and we buy it, get under it—and this keeps us sinning in the same areas. Don't let the fear of condemnation stop you. We must be able to face up to what is ensnaring us and *trust* our Father with our confession, our repentance, and our renunciation of these spiritual S&M gadgets that, ironically enough, bring us some payoff or pleasure as they beat us into submission (or we wouldn't keep going back to them).

To that point, psychology 101 tells us that we are pleasure/pain creatures. We are payoff motivated. And yes, pain can bring pleasure for some. (Don't laugh or shake your head in amazement. Make your own list first.) When we indulge in painful sin, something in us is being fed, spiritually and emotionally, that keeps us going back, like crack addicts, to the very sin that keeps us from our promises as God's daughters. (Eternal life isn't the only promise God offers us, by the way. It's a pretty awesome one, but joy, peace, power, and abundance are a few more of the goodies that our awesome kingdom offers and that our pleasurable pain keeps us from.)

Condemnation, if we let it, will control us. I once heard that some people never feel good unless they feel bad. Get it? In other words, some of us feel that the only way to be loved by God is to wallow miserably in our guilt and confession. But a spirit of guilt, as we noted, drives us right back to the things that keep us on the devil's hamster wheel—while he holds the cheese just out of our reach and accuses us to our Father that we never reach it!

I can tell you as a parent that if my daughter kept coming to me confessing the same old stuff after we had been over it, after I had pardoned her and loved her and accepted her in spite of her yuck, I would at some point release her to the consequence of her continued agreement with her sin. We have to confess our sin—and then choose life. Israel was given the choice in Deuteronomy 30:19, and we are given the choice today.

Good Girls

So you've made your list. Now what?

Repent. Now's the time. Take that list, confess your sin to your Fiancé, and start walking the road of righteousness. If we confess our sin, God is faithful and just to forgive us and to cleanse us from all unrighteousness (see 1 John 1:9). That word "just" in 1 John 1:9 means exactly that, as in justice. God's justice has been served—on our Fiancé. Jesus is the One who paid for all the world's whoredom: "God . . . hath reconciled us to himself by Jesus Christ" (2 Cor. 5:18).

Trust. It is imperative that we plant our flag in the rock of truth that He is faithful and will forgive us, heal us, and make us whole.

Accept. Accepting that we are heard, understood, forgiven, and cleansed can be a real challenge for some of us. But accepting *His* acceptance of us is crucial to not returning to our sin.

"But will my repentance, trust, and acceptance of God's forgiveness stick?" you might ask. "I've tried before and failed."

If you've been in church very long, you've likely heard of appropriating the blood of Jesus in our lives. What does that mean, exactly? What does it look like? In its simplest form (in Monica lingo), it means that we decide to believe what God says about us, and we step on anything that feels, thinks, or speaks to the contrary (see Eph. 2:6). We speak directly to those revealed patterns of lower-level thinking, feeling, and living, and we declare the truth over them and stand. We turn from anything contrary to the life promised to us and run like mad to the safety of our Father (see Ps. 91).

Once we've gained this knowledge of repentance and confession and appropriation and started applying it, we're on the path to dealing with our cycles of whoredom, once and for all. But even then, it isn't a downhill ride.

For starters, upon our turning away from our sin in repentance and appropriating the blood of the Lamb, all hell will rise up to tell us that it is not possible. It will whisper that it is futile, that we will, in fact, die. Or that we are once and for all saved, so what's the big deal?

Besides the enemy opposition, we beat ourselves up. It's not always easy for us to receive mercy. Many of my friends say things to try to feel better about their fear of potential judgment, such as "What goes around comes around." But when we sit and commiserate with quirky sayings like that, we are in direct alignment with our enemy and *not* in fellowship with our kingdom. Sure, what we sow, we reap, but how many things have we sown that, *thank God*, never sprouted? I wonder if that's because He honored someone's prayer to pardon us. I don't subscribe to karma for one reason: she is merciless. I can't afford to believe in that mess, because, frankly, I need mercy too badly.

Thankfully, unlike karma and the universe (the world's new favorite term for our Father), the living and true God of Abraham, Isaac, and Jacob, also known as Love, keeps no record of wrongs (see 1 Cor. 1:13). He just doesn't. It is written. Don't argue with me—tell your devils, in His name, to take it up with Him. (I have to send the ones assigned to me to His throne regularly.)

We still have the "being of sin"—our flesh—to deal with (see Rom. 7:17). Paul makes it clear that even when we want to do right, we don't always do it but quite the contrary. We have the being of sin that dwells within us to thank for that.

That might make us feel as if the odds are stacked against us. But we simply need a deeper revelation of the power of God's mercy and grace and of our Daddy's and our Fiancé's heart toward us (see Ps. 136). We need to see exactly what was completed at that cross and in the resurrection of Christ. God wants us to see ourselves through His eyes, through Their eyes. We can do this! But *not without Them*.

When we embrace Their view of us, we can live from that higher place. We are no longer slaves to sin, to lower-level living. When we walk in relationship with Them, we can be good.

I have to admit that something about being known as a "good girl" fluffs my flesh. Not sure why. Maybe it's because that little James Dean-like character that resonates within me gets stoked or maybe because most "good girls" I've known were, um, let's say, less than holy, while those of us who happened to dress not so conservatively were dubbed otherwise. Dunno. But Dad has a few things to say about our being good.

It's time to remind ourselves of who we were created to be from the beginning. When God made us, we were the gleam in our heavenly Daddy's eye, remember? We were awesome! "God saw *every thing* that he had made"—that included man—"and, behold, it was *very good*" (Gen. 1:31).

So God made Monica, and He saw her and said, "She is *very good.*" Stop right here and insert your name. Do it! Tell that unloving, anti-Christ (anti-love) spirit that doesn't believe it to leave you be, in Jesus' name, and just say it. Out loud! Not once but three times. Ready?

"In the beginning God made _____ [you, my beautifully awesome sister], and He saw me and said, 'She. is. very. good.'" Got it? God *said* that about *you*! Pretty amazing. And all God's children said, "Amen!"

As we talked about in course 1, many of us in the church were raised to think that we humans aren't much more than Adam's horrific choice until Jesus comes along. And even *with* Jesus some circles subscribe to the pathetic "unworthy" gospel. Leave it to a spirit of religion, spearheaded in the enemy's kingdom, to share the good news of Jesus while making us believe that we are too sludgy to ever deserve it, much less enjoy it. Sick.

True enough, we did nothing, zero, zip, to deserve anything good from God (see Eph. 2:8–9). And yes, our righteousness is as filthy rags (see Isa. 64:6). Seriously. But that is *not* His heart toward us now (thanks to our Fiancé), nor was it His heart when They first created us (see Gen. 1:31). I mean, yes, our self-righteousness still stinks in His nostrils, because in it we are basically saying, "Yeah, hey, thanks for Jesus, but I got this." Not exactly accepting His love. The it's-all-about-us-and-our-works attitude doesn't make for a happy Dad. But there's more to the story.

In spite of our fallen nature, you will notice that the Godhead has always left a few of us human spirit-beings here on earth (even as few as eight one time; see Gen. 6:6–8; 7:11–13). He could have annihilated (and nearly did) the entire human race, but I personally believe that They didn't because They have *hope* for Their creation. That includes you and me. Again, our Fiancé is proof of that. So settle it once and for all in your being that you are fearfully and wonderfully made and that God says you *are* good. And in that truth you can *be* good.

Cleansing Your Palate

- What would you say your number-one draw into sin is? (List lust items.)

- List any area(s) of your life in which you feel held captive.

- What are your beliefs about Satan?

- What is your idea of repentance?

- What do think about Jesus' sacrifice on the cross? How does it make you feel?

- List any areas in your life in which you may be creepin' (sneaking around).

- What is your understanding of grace? What is your understanding of mercy?

- Do you believe that you are good?

DIG A LITTLE DEEPER

Look up Hosea 4:6, James 4:8–10, and 2 Timothy 2:25, and share with your sisters or write down what each passage says about what can happen when we reject God's law.

Course 4

Addicted to Love

It is better to trust in the LORD *than to put confidence in man.*

PSALM 118:8

Addictions. You know it. We all have them.

I heard the trash truck coming through the hood a few weeks ago, and when I looked out—wow! Mr. If We Had a Calendar for Trash Men, He Would Be on the Cover was riding on the back of the truck with the body of Mr. Universe. No shirt on, tan, and flexing! Ha! I was like, what the heck?! Seriously, he was *out of place*. I felt like David must have when he looked at Bathsheba. *Yikes*! (I can't say I've ever been into trash men, but this one was appealing to the eyes.)

So my daughter—a seventeen-year-old, hormonally equipped young woman trying to walk after the Spirit of God—comes home later that day and says, "Mom! Did you see the trash guy?!" We burst into laughter, giggling incessantly for several minutes.

But in our laughter I had a moment of clarity, and my spirit man rose up, stopped, and reminded *both of us* that the men we "appreciate" (gawk at and get all giggly about) are our *brothers* first. They are His *sons* first. (Of course, some of them aren't yet, but viewing them this way keeps our heads in the right place.)

Now listen, I'm not saying that we can't admire God's gorgeous creatures (and I will never not think that Chris Helmsworth is a beautiful creation), but there is a difference between in gratitude simply acknowledging someone's beauty and devouring men in our minds. When we want a guy, we act differently: we straighten our backs, suck in our tummies, and pretend we don't know that he's there. We pay more attention than we should.

The problem is, if we let this play out in our hearts and minds, our spirit leads us nowhere but goofy-decisionville.

We go to bed with him on our minds, and for some of us, before we know it, our thoughts lead to action—and we start *taking* from someone who doesn't even have a say-so in the matter. Yes, the M word. Masturbation.

When people ask me my thoughts on this subject, I'm like, "Well" (insert Monica theology), "what are you thinking about while doing it? It's not like you're thinking of mowing the lawn or smelling a rose or enjoying a sunset *alone*. It's like spiritual theft. You're enjoying someone who hasn't even said yes." The person isn't present with his own will, and when we think about it that way, masturbation is kinda creepy.

I also know that in the times when this has become a struggle for me, it's usually because I need some kind of comfort, usually after a rejection. (Maybe it stems from my childhood, I don't know, but I see a direct correlation between feeling like I'm garbage after a perceived or real rejection and engaging in self-comfort.)

Then again, sometimes I'm just a forty-something-year-old woman with hormones who gets carried away with thoughts, and I'm mad as anything that God hasn't dropped that hotty Boaz in my bed (see Ruth 4). Before I know it, I have a new mental husband in a flash.

You may not be convicted and you might rock on, but that's my take on it—masturbation is basically spiritual and mental fornication (I hate that word). If you are married and doing it and your husband's shiny face isn't the one you see in your head, it's called adultery. Sorry. We don't need a concordance-driven Bible study of the ancient texts or the lost scrolls. It's pretty simple. And for those who summon the Holy Spirit while doing it, I'm just going to refer you to ministry, and quickly. No condemnation, but nothing could be further from the purpose and character of our Father's Spirit.

Don't gasp, ladies, women do this regularly. Again, our enemy is insane and longs to pervert every good thing that our Father created. Make no mistake—sex is super good, but only when birthed in proper order. When it's not, it can very easily become an addiction.

We like to think that men are the only ones with issues regarding lust and the big stare down, but let's be real, ladies, we are just more subtle at our attempts to soak in the fullness of someone's gorgeousness. Those of us well versed in this dance of manipulation may go on to strategically place our masks (or our breasts) in the off chance that we can rope him in with something other than who we are. But remember, ladies, as I tell my daughter, how you get 'em is how you gotta keep 'em. True story.

Where Do You Get Your Worth?

According to Webster's, an addiction is "a strong and harmful need to regularly have something (such as a drug) or do something (such as gamble)." It can apply just as easily to our desire for approval or sex or love.

I'm thankful for the check in my spirit that day with the Fabio trash-man dude, because it ministered to me, and I was able to minister to my daughter, about the beauty of propriety. Being appropriate because we *are* appropriate is a new concept to many of us. It's different from behavior modification due to fear of consequences or human perception. Being appropriate is confidently living from our highest nature (righteousness), being fulfilled and still feeling desirable and, well, sexy.

This is important when that little hissing serpent comes in the form of feelings, comparison, lies, self-pity, or accusation toward

God for taking so long. Or when Mr. Always Smells Good—who has told you how mean his wife is—bends down at your desk to say a simple hi. I could write another book on that, but I digress. Again, our feelings, in and of themselves, are not bad. Only when we live solely by them—when we are driven by them and manipulated with them—do they become a liability. An addiction.

Living in the state of mind that the men around us are *siblings first* will keep us from choosing men who *aren't* his sons (yet) or who say they love Jesus but don't know what it means to be a son of God. A man need not be perfect to be a good partner and visionary in life, but dating someone who needs you to be his "holy spirit" and drag him to his own well is exhausting. Girl, please.

Using a man to put a stamp of approval on our existence and worth and desirability is *not* a better meal. And the word "using" is paramount, because when lust disguises itself as an innocent heart desire, we do in fact use people. (Remember the M convo?) The poor guy we drool over has no idea that we've just chosen him to be our savior and validation to our life as a woman.

Remember, lust takes. Love gives and receives. We place the guy of our desires on our never-able-to-attain expectation wheel (which every man will cheerfully climb onto for a brief challenge, since men are born with internal superhero capes). But when he is faced with repeated failures in a role he was never intended to attain, much less sustain, we end up just as lonely, frustrated, and desperate as we were to begin with—but now with kids and mortgages and the crumbling identity we tried to create for everyone around us and for ourselves. Eek.

We need to return to the well. We need filling from Jesus.

We *are* whole. Remember? If we *knew* that, we would yoke ourselves with men who are also growing and whole.

My advice to you is exactly what I am asking Dad to help me do in my man-weeding process: seek not only His approval but head straight to your spiritual covering (pastors), family, and friends with any new male possibilities. For one reason: to see if this guy is teachable and humble and if he is interested in fellowship with others in the body and with the people you love. In a multitude of counselors there is safety (see Prov. 11:14).

The horizontal aspect of our faith (relationship with likeminded believers) is as important as the vertical (relationship with our Fiancé and our Dad and the Holy Spirit). We like to think otherwise, but I've learned more about our Father's heart on the horizontal level than by living in accusation and autonomy toward the body of Christ. Invite sound people to guide you or simply confirm what the Lord has spoken to you regarding the single-most important decision that you will make as a single woman entertaining sharing the garden of your heart.

Don't get me wrong—hopefully, he's all the godly qualities above *and* hot. But hotness alone hasn't gotten me anywhere but burned. Ouch.

My pastors remind me that I'm in my Abba Father's house. And so are you. As long as we are still single (betrothed to Jesus, but not yet married to Him), we are afforded the covering, wisdom, and care in our Father's house that married women have (in theory) from a husband. We would be wise to exercise that position and truth.

Missionary This

We've talked about missionary dating. You know, when we date that super-hot, thoughtful, successful guy who always smells amazing, who just gets us, who went to church as a child and believes in God but feels that he can experience God in the woods on Sunday morning? The guy we just know will suddenly drop all his worldly ways to find the Jesus of his youth again for us? Yeah. *That* guy. Well, missionary dating is what we do when we're addicted to love. And I'm the queen of it. And the fact that I'm a single woman writing this book should tell you how successful that's been for me. Ha.

Why do we go after guys we *know* aren't pursuing the life we want? When it comes to *my* lust list, the Lord has shown me a few reasons why I, Monica, have chosen to date non-believers: It's not just because I had seen as many wacky things in my brothers in Christ as in the world. It's also because I believed that God was impotent—so I also believed that man was. And when we think guys can't lead, guess who gets to be on the throne to make sure that all goes well? Guess who becomes the spiritual leader and missionary martyr that we vehemently deny we want to be? Yep, *us*. Sure, it's empowering. And yeah, it satisfies our addiction for love. But it's *exhausting*.

Many of my friends do this too. But being the spiritually strong one at the expense of proper order and covering ends in devastating results. If the wedding is the goal, don't forget that there will be a *marriage* to cultivate and maintain. Order is crucial. It may feel great to have a guy who "needs" you, but this kind of husband ends up being the equivalent of an additional child. If you choose this route, you will sit over coffee complaining that he never does this or that and that you are responsible for everything. Remember, ladies, how you get em' is how you gotta keep em'. I'm just telling you.

Just because you can be superwoman as a single lady doesn't mean that this is the prescribed order of the marriage you would like to someday have. Sure, we can open our own door, think for ourselves, and do many things on our own, but if a man is in our life, we want to relish the opportunity to actually let him *be* one. Remember—*order*.

I fed my addictions because I *believed* but didn't *know* that God, my Daddy, *is* concerned, near and capable. Instead I needed to say, "Okay, I'm gonna say yes to Your Son's invite to our engagement and trust where, what, and who You bring me to."

A man who *finds* a wife finds a good thing (see Prov. 18:22). That means that the guy does the finding, while we stay busy getting to know our Fiancé and ourselves. Our Dad, whose house we live in, is busy watching over His Word to perform it (see Jer. 1:12). He tells us, "Seek ye first the kingdom of God, and his righteousness; and all these things"—including a partner, husband, visionary—"shall be added unto to you" (Matt. 6:33). (Woot. Delight yourself in the Lord, and *He* will give you the desires of your heart. Take a look at Psalm 37:4.)

Dear Jesus, Help!

Back to the hunks of dust—for we are but dust (see Ps. 103:14).

An innocent desire turned lust can be defined simply as this: worshiping the dust God made (men). When we do this, we agree with an accusation toward God that He is not supplying what we want when we want it. Therefore, we *take* what we want. In turn, we end up in self-idolatry, because our way is better, and after all, we have needs. Just ask Hollywood or any chick magazine.

Because we don't know how to love without fear (see 1 John 4:18), we sometimes worship the created thing (man) out of fear. That is not only defeating but simply and completely unnecessary. Our Fiancé reminds us and assures us that we are not alone in our plight and are in fact, understood, heard, cared for, and even pitied as a father pities his child (see Ps. 103:13). He also warns us of the futility of placing our hopes and trust in man (including ourselves). (That does not mean that He's saying not to trust men. Gotta keep things context.)

Our Fiancé addresses our hearts clearly regarding those issues that every single woman eventually wonders about through endless nights of tears, loneliness, illicit sheets, ridiculous and costly decisions, friends' wedding and newborns. (*You know* those events you go to, whether never married or divorced or widowed, with a bright smile, dressed all cute with your strappy heals and new clutch—just in case some single Boaz is in attendance—while that little naggy voice says, "Hmm, why did *she* get such a blessing? What's wrong with *me*? When will it be *my* turn?" Or the best of the lying voices for us Christian girls, "She must be holier than me. " That's my personal fav.)

Have no fear, sisters! We are all in the same boat (see Eph. 6:12)! Those little devils of comparison, envy, accusation, fear? They speak to *all* of us (see James 3:14–16). If we would but turn to our Fiancé in these times of battle (sitting with our legs crossed with a smile on our face with WWIII going on in our head *is* a battle), we would hear Him say, "Hi, sweetheart! I know that the enemy is raging—he did the same thing to Me [see Matt. 4:1–11]! I know *exactly* how you feel [see Heb. 4:15], and I'm so glad that you came to visit Me today! I am so proud of you and your decision to trust Me—to choose Me and our life together!" He would bend down and pour His words of life into our quickly emptying jar of hope: "I *am* on your side" (see Ps. 118:6). He would go on to say, "Do not fear: what can man do unto you? It is better to trust in Me, the Lord, than to put your confidence in man" (see Ps. 118:8).

Ahhhh . . . music to our ears, water for our soul, a bullet in our arsenal, the sharpening of our sword, the helmet of our salvation, the peace on our feet, the covering of our heart in righteousness, and a girdle to keep us on the right path, the Botox to our furrowed brow (see Eph. 6:13–16). You know what I'm sayin'.

By the way, these little devils of comparison, fear, worry, dread, accusation, and jealousy are equal-opportunity invaders of our spiritual space (see Luke 11:24–26) and eventually of our minds, and they land us right back in stupid-decisionville. When we follow their voices, we look like them, act like them, and speak like them. We are *not* them. Why give them any of our personal real estate?

This is our Fiancé, ladies: He's personal, He's real, He's present, He's available (ha, now there's a change), He loves us, He desires us, He has hope for us, He covers us, He listens to all our whining, and He *understands* us!

He protects us (see John 8:1–11). He longs for us. He makes our crooked, worn-out paths straight (see Isa. 45:2). By God's Holy Spirit Jesus speaks to us and edifies us through His Word, because He *is* the Word (see John 1:1). He gives us grace (*divine influence on our hearts*), He imparts mercy, He equips us to do this thing called salvation and abundant living. *He is for us*. He's not a theory or a belief system. He's a living, breathing, feeling being—He's *alive* (see Ps. 46:1).

You say, "It sure doesn't *feel* that way sometimes!" Since we went there, let's go there.

Capturing Feelings and Thoughts

Yep. At times, my feelings have a special button that has Satan's finger on it. I envision these moments of temptation: I can see his badly manicured, hairy finger hitting the button, and this fabulous tower erects from the dust of the ground with the banner above it, in big *National Lampoon* lights, reads "MONICA'S FEELINGS." Bejeweled and glittering with every lie of the enemy, he keeps it shiny with *self*-everything: pity, loathing, righteousness (he's a real sweetie, and he knows me), comparison, a record of my wrongs, rejection, abasement, exaltation, protection, doubt, entitlement. He is a faithful landlord of selfdom.

If I don't hit the eject button or send a distress call to my Dad, who in turn summons His Spirit and shows up with my Fiancé, I'm in deep doo-doo.

Seriously. It's bad. And it doesn't take long to happen. That's why it's so important for us to know the Word. Because Jesus *is* the Word. How can we allow Him to speak into our situation if we don't know it?! Read your Bibles, ladies.

In an age of yoga and letting our minds be "free" from thought, I offer a contradictory solution to our raging feelings based on the Word: we are instructed to take *every* thought captive (see 2 Cor. 10:5). That means that *we* have to *do* something (see James 1:22). We have to be aware of our thoughts, not void of them or breathing and repeating mantras to ourselves in order to fool ourselves into thinking that we can escape them. Um, no.

Breathing is great. Slowly inhaling and exhaling is fab. Our cells love it. But leaving our minds open to every spiritual Tom, Dick, and Harry? Not our kingdom's way.

Doing (practicing) the Word can appear exhausting. But so is trying to say "ohm" with your legs over your head without a single thought. Just sayin'. Taking every. single. thought. captive is *work*. At least in the beginning. But we can rest in one of God's sweet everythings—His promises—that as we bring our thoughts into agreement with our Dad (submit) and resist our enemy, the devil *will* flee (see James 4:7). Selfdom is conquered in that very moment, and we get to show up as our authentic selves: His daughters, dressed in righteousness and beauty galore!

We are desirable, particularly to ourselves, when we *are* ourselves. Not to mention, men find a woman who enjoys and loves herself basically the cat's meow. It means that you won't look to him to tell you who you are. *Freedom.*

As time goes on in our practice of the Word, our thoughts *become one* (there's that knowing thing again) with our Fiancé, and we don't have to *work* at bringing these things into captivity. They end up being like the creepy dude who flirts with you when you have an excellent boyfriend: you recognize creepy immediately and want no part of it. And *nothing* that the enemy tells us is short of creepy (see John 8:44). No matter the spin he puts on it, if it doesn't line up with the sweet everythings that our Fiancé whispers to us, it's gotta go.

Here's why: science has shown that whatever we don't take captive in our thought life will rule us psychologically and subsequently physiologically. This is the essence of addiction.

The Science of Blessings and Curses

See, we are all wired with a need to be loved, because we were birthed *in* love. (Love that.) But when we perceive that our needs are not being met by life, people, encounters, or positions, we become easy prey for the enemy of our souls. His whispers to us of discontentment are usually not loud and seem somewhat innocuous (see Gen. 3:1), but here's what happens on a physiological level when we aren't filling up from our true cistern, Jesus.

A cycle begins, and over time it wears a literal pathway in our brain that causes lower-level living to kick into full gear and take over. When we *take* out of lust, whether we grab at men or success or anything else, we literally create what I call a "crave pattern" in our bodies.

Then, when those things aren't fed, we literally feel the loss, anxiety, and despair, much like a drug addict, which leads us back to stupid-decisionville. *Unless*, of course, we stop at the well long enough to establish the proper order of our desires, assert the mind of Christ, and set our will to *live* patiently, wholly, and holy for our best life, which *is* His will. (Notice that I didn't say *wait*. This may just be a Monica thing, but something about that word stirs my flesh. It seems so stagnant to wait—if by waiting, that is, we mean simply languishing in our loneliness and doing nothing productive—as it offers an excuse not to *live* while waiting. It implies that somehow my life as a single woman can't be whole until I have a mate or success, and *that* is definitely not truth.)

When we drink from the well of *living* water and begin to starve the old pathways, the brain is physiologically transformed with new neural pathways, and our old life becomes just that—*old* (see Rom. 12:1–2; Eph. 4:22–24; 5:26–27). Not without a fight, of course. But persistence is key, and you will prevail, because *He* said so.

I'd like to offer some empirical scientific proof regarding this addiction loop and *the* way out to freedom.

When we have developed a pattern of doing things our way, particularly in the area of love, we are easy pickin's for addiction to set in. Addiction not only leads to physical, psychological, and emotional disease, but it sets a subpar standard of our relationships with God, ourselves, and others.

Researchers have found the following:

Intense feelings of romantic love affect the brain in the same way drugs like cocaine or powerful pain relievers do.

"The reason people are so attracted to cocaine is that it activates the area of the brain that makes you feel good," researcher Arthur Aron, PhD, tells WebMD. "The same reward area is activated when people are experiencing the intense desire of romantic love." . . .

[Aron and colleague Sean Mackey, MD, PhD, hypothesize] *that love affected the brain in the same way many addictive drugs do*, by targeting the "feel good" chemical in the brain known as dopamine. This reward system has also been shown to be critical in *pain management.*[1]

Another study shows,

Addiction is a brain disease. As a person's reward circuitry becomes increasingly dulled and desensitized by drugs, nothing else can compete with them—food, family, and friends lose their relative value, while the ability to curb the need to seek and use drugs evaporates. Ironically and cruelly, eventually even the drug loses its ability to reward, but the compromised brain leads addicted people to pursue it, anyway; the memory of the drug has become more powerful than the drug itself. . . .

In fact, environmental variables such as stress or drug exposure can cause lasting changes to genes and their function, known as epigenetic changes, which can result in long-term changes to brain circuits.[2]

A review of *New York Times* business writer Charles Duhigg's book, *The Power of Habit*, states,

Every habit starts with a psychological pattern called a "habit loop," which is a three-part process. First, there's a cue, or trigger, that tells your brain to go into automatic mode and let a behavior unfold. . . .

Neuroscientists have traced our habit-making behaviors to a part of the brain called the basal ganglia, which also plays a key role in the development of emotions, memories and pattern recognition. Decisions, meanwhile, are made in a different part of the brain called the prefrontal cortex. But as soon as a behavior becomes automatic, the decision-making part of your brain goes into a sleep mode of sorts.

"In fact, the brain starts working less and less," says Duhigg. "The brain can almost completely shut down."[3]

Finally, research from Dr. Petris Levounis, director of the Addiction Institute of New York at St. Luke's and Roosevelt Hospitals in Manhattan, shows us,

In normal patients, dopamine plays a major role in motivation and reward, surging before and during a pleasurable activity—say, eating or sex—to make patients want to repeat a behavior that's crucial to the survival of the species.

Dopaminergic pathways connect the limbic system, which is responsible for emotion, with the hippocampus, which is responsible for memory. This combination etches rewarding behaviors into the brain with strong, even seductive, memories.

The problem arises when the memory and the craving to recapture it take over a person's life.

"Imagine what a stronghold these highjacked pleasure reward pathways take on our brains and our whole existence when they're so closely connected geographically and anatomically speaking with our memories and our emotions," Levounis, says. . . .

"Ultimately," Levounis says, "the war on drugs is a war between the highjacked pleasure reward pathways that push the person to want to use, and the frontal lobes, which try to keep the beast at bay. That is the essence of addiction."[4]

Notice that the final quote uses the word "stronghold." Strongholds are *not* of our Father, and when they get hold of us, it's a clear indicator that something other than ourselves (see Eph. 6:12) is influencing us and our ability to walk in freedom. Once we are aware that spiritual powers are trying to trap us, we have the right to actively, out loud, bring that thing or thought into captivity of the light, say "No thanks," and book it outta there!

You may be wondering, *Why out loud?* Well, the spirit world is no joke. It is alive. Other spirit beings besides us exist, according to our Fiancé, and they aren't all holy. One third of them fell. As spirit beings ourselves, we communicate spiritually (through theta brainwaves), and while it's a sweet, comforting gesture to believe that as born-again Christians, God is the only one broadcasting on that frequency, that's simply not the case. Just ask the apostle Peter—Jesus once addressed the devil while directly conversing with Peter (see Matt. 16:21–23). Or better yet, look no further than your own thought life, and tell me that everything in your mind is from God. This is super important to our freedom. If we don't know by whom we are being held captive, it will be nearly impossible for us to do proper battle, and usually we end up believing wrongly that *we* are our own enemies. This is false doctrine.

While our minds, bodies, and souls are influenced through our spirit, Satan's kingdom cannot hear our thoughts. The devil and demons can see our reactions and actions, but our thoughts, thankfully, are a one-way communication avenue when it comes to God's kingdom and to the devils assigned to do their work against and through us (see Luke 22:3). (Don't go exorcist on me just yet— although I *have* witnessed interesting manifestations of spirits in Christians; see Luke 11:24.)[5]

I find that when a particular naggy thought won't leave me and I *know* that it's not of my Father's kingdom or from the breath of my Fiancé, I'm like, "Okay, all of ya'll get in the car, come on! We're goin' to see my Dad, and you *know* if *He* deals with you, it's gonna be a bad day for you guys" (see Heb. 4:16).

Needless to say, when I do that, those impressions, feelings, and thoughts that are tempting me through my spirit man (theta) quickly dissipate. They are a pain to deal with, but one thing they are not is unintelligent. *They* know who our Daddy is. The question is, do *we*? They know their position in creation and eternity—do *we*? They know our authority in Christ—do *we*? For many of us, the answer is no. How do I know this? Less-than-abundant living.

When self rises in the form of feelings that want to lead you in direct opposition of the higher-living (righteous) path, cry out! I'm not talking about denial. On the contrary, facing strongholds head on is about as *present* as one can be while living in hope and authority. This is higher living—abundantly.

Welfare Mentality—and the Way Out

The book of Ephesians addresses a group of people who had *forgotten* who and whose they were. Because of that they lived as beggars, as it were.

We do the same thing. In fact, it's why we settle for the lusty life.

Having lived on survivor's benefits since my husband's death, I can tell you with certainty that the welfare system is designed, spiritually and otherwise, to keep an otherwise healthy, capable child of God oppressed by compromise to the detriment of his or her own purposes and dreams. Even though my daughter was ill and I could not leave her unattended, it's also true that the obvious and most cost-effective choice and temptation for me as a semi-college-educated woman was to stay put. I'm grateful for the assistance and not sure what we have done without it, but God is a God of restoration, and when He restores, we have the right to walk in that restoration—and turn in our WIC card.[6]

As a welfare recipient, however, it can feel as if we stand to lose more than we gain by leaving the system. I liken some of my newly divorced sisters to this mentality, particularly ones with alimony. I've seen it time and time again. A woman is suddenly divorced, whether by her choice or not, and alimony is in place to sustain her for a period of time. But when she is faced with alimony going bye-bye, I can't tell you the unreal choices she makes in the way of panic to ensure her financial security. It is truly grievous. She goes from cradle robbing to dating old guys—what I call "walker dating"—running to anything that represents security. But seriously.

In these times of global financial uncertainty coupled with the whispers of war, it's *rough* being a single woman if we aren't looking up. This really boils down to a trust-versus-fear issue, an issue of knowing who and whose we are not just in the life to come but *now*.

I'm outing us on this, because it's worthy of outing. That we have to live as orphans is a fear-born lie that the enemy uses to get us to make agreements for our lives never intended by our Dad. How do I know? Because fear is in the driver's seat.

Security becomes our idol, and the hunk of dust is the facilitator.

Get off the spiritual welfare cheese, ladies, of an ex-husband or ex-boyfriend who shoulda, coulda, woulda. Get out of the "I'll just chill for a while 'cause he owes me anyway" mind-set, or quit behaving like the never been marrieds who are just hanging out with different guys until the right one comes along. Instead inquire of your Dad as to what *your* life means.

Use your gifts and talents to move forward, and by all means, forgive the past. If you don't, the past will accompany you everywhere you go. It will show up at every interview, invade every blind date, and override every Botox injection you could possibly pay for. Bitterness is not our calling and neither is mediocrity. The world needs what He created you to offer.

One day I walked into a high-end department store in Atlanta and was instantly captivated by one of the most beautiful women I have ever seen. She was tall and thin, had long, healthy hair, and modeled tanned, shiny skin. My first thought was, *It must be nice to be a kept woman.*

But I've learned, in all my years of singlehood and pursuing righteousness, where my beauty resides. When my eyes are fixed on Him, when I live in my talents and gifts, serving the body of Christ, I literally glow. (As a matter of fact, one evening as I edited this book, a man told me I was glowing. I knew he wasn't kidding; I felt it. When we are on purpose and in fellowship with our Father and our Light of the world, we can't help but shine.) I couldn't pay for this type of beauty treatment if I tried. It surpasses my income and circumstances and bears a direct witness to the truth of Isaiah 26:3: "Thou wilt keep him in perfect peace, whose mind is stayed on thee: because he trusteth in thee."

I am not a beggar, dependent on whatever feeds my additions. I am a kept woman, living in my Father's house. I am kept in perfect peace. I am kept from harm and from many damaging things. And so are you.

Cleansing Your Palate

- What do you think of men?

- What do you think men were created for?

- Do you believe that Jesus is your husband?

- Can you think of any "little lies" that you may be holding on to for comfort or hope?

- Have you ever known love without fear? Describe it.

- How much rule do your feelings have in your life?

DIG A LITTLE DEEPER

Look up Psalm 37:4, Proverbs 11:14, and Matthew 6:33, and share with your sisters or write down what each passage says about how you can break any addictions you may have and about the rewards of loving God more than anything else.

Course 5

Annulment, Please

If a woman also vow a vow unto the LORD, and bind herself by a bond, being in her father's house. . . if her father disallow her in the day that he heareth; not any of her vows, or of her bonds wherewith she hath bound her soul, shall stand: and the LORD shall forgive her, because her father disallowed her.

NUMBERS 30:3-5

Our Dad has much to say about vows. He honors them. Especially *His* (see a big one in Gen. 3:15). He also takes us at *our* word, and guess who else does? Yep. The agent of the fall of man, that abusive father of lies, our enemy, Satan.

As I investigated this thing that we call vows, or promises or oaths, I found that King David proclaimed that he would rise early and pay his vows unto the Lord and praise Him (see Ps. 116:14; 119:147). And in Numbers 30 we see that vows are a pretty serious matter. God says that if a man or a woman makes a vow to Him, he or she needs to keep it.

Interesting, though, to note that God gives a prescription for a woman's vows to be disavowed. If a woman's father or husband heard her vow and disagreed with it, her vow had to go, God released her from it.

Though not usually under such formal circumstances, we too make vows—with ourselves, with others, and with God. And as single girls living in our Father's house, when we makes vows in our Dad's hearing that we should not be making, He can override them. That's good news, ladies.

I can personally attest to making a vow to God that I definitely could not pay or keep. Not a good place to be. Enemy accusation territory numero uno.

I also remember making vows in judgment of others—I would *never* do that or *be* like them (whoever "them" might be). Well, let me tell you, doing this bites us. If our vow is based on someone else's failures, and in judgment we declare that we will never be like that person, we can rest assured that our vow will eventually come back to visit us in some form or fashion. Our Fiancé tells us that by whatever measure we judge, we will be met with the same judgment (see Matt. 7:2). Amen or ouch? (I'm a witness to this truth. Ouch.)

There's a big difference between seeing behavior that we don't care to emulate and in a spirit of mercy choosing to agree with God's Word for our own life to subvert that path and sitting around the water cooler casting stones from our glass house, whether internally or as we commiserate with others.

Our words are recorded in the heavenlies (see Matt. 12:36). They have the power of life and death (see Prov. 18:21). When we as single women wander from the well of our Fiancé, the vows we make hinder us, bind us, and lock us into ways of thinking, feeling, and acting that God never intended for us.

Unequally Yoked

The vows we make as single women can be many. Maybe you have vowed to never end up poor or alone like your sister or your mother. Perhaps you've vowed never to marry a man like your earthly father or your best friend's husband. Maybe you have vowed never to be hurt or vulnerable again.

But the number-one vow that I see my fellow single sisters making, no matter their age, race, or denomination, is that of giving their heart to someone who hasn't asked them for it or to someone completely incapable of nurturing and covering a woman's heart.

You know the vow I'm talking about, the one that tells you to share your body or total heart and mind with him before he's asked you to join him in covenant. The one that drives you to decorate *his* home in anticipation of your color patterns. The one that makes you think you have a right to know his whereabouts at all times and whom he's out with (because you are his quasi wife). The vow that gets you to leave your kids at night to be with the man you "love."

Don't gasp in judgment. We girls do some crazy, irrational, downright evil things to honor our vows. But make no mistake—these vows are birthed from broken walls in the city of our soul.

Any man who is willing to allow you, a vessel of honor (see 2 Tim. 2:21), to travel down these vow paths is in fact playing. He is playing with your heart, your mind, and your very identity, at least on a soul level. He has zero equipping to cover, love, respect, and honor a vessel of God the way God's Word tells a man to do (see Eph. 5:25). Buy him a blankie, pray from a distance, and move on.

See, when we said yes to our Father through the blood of our Fiancé, we became alive to Him as His Spirit-birthed daughters (more on this in the next course of this meal). We *belong* to Him. He bought us back from our enemy and death. He is our Father (see Rom. 8:15). Abba, Daddy, Father.

Our enemy, however, still lays claim to us by virtue of our lack of knowledge (see Hos. 4:6) and wisdom, and for some of us, a willful disregard for our adoptive Father's ways. This usually stems from lack of intimacy with our Daddy because of not knowing who He is—which means that we don't who *we* are. The enemy doesn't give up so readily. He has something great at stake: his pride and your soul (your mind, will, and emotions).

He wants every aspect of us in order to us *his* future—his plans for our life and for our generations. But it's not personal, ladies; he hates our Daddy (see Isa. 14:13). As my former pastor teaches, we are in the middle of a family feud that started many moons ago, and since we are part of the Spirit family and have chosen to say yes to our Daddy's invitation to be adopted, Satan hates us. Simple. (Hence my ministry apparel line, SHYwear—Satan Hates Us.)

The good news is that our Daddy has great hopes for us as His daughters. At the very least, He's hoping that we will eat and digest His Word, which instructs us that light and darkness have nothing to do with each other and that being unequally yoked is just that: unequal (see 2 Cor. 6:14). Instruction is part of good parenting. And our Father is a good Dad.

Get a real picture of two oxen attached at the neck and shoulders, plowing. Now imagine the guy you're dating or engaged to strapped in next you. Are the two of you pulling in the same direction (see Amos 3:3)?

If not, *unlatch*, *release*, and re-hitch to your Fiancé. Immediately. His "yoke is easy, and [His] burden is light" (Matt. 11:30). A much better and satisfying yokemate, wouldn't you say?

Tell your enemy no thanks to the selfdom throne that he will erect with every good excuse he feeds you not to run from your guy. If you find yourself confused, call your elders or church leaders or a trusted friend, receive counsel (see Prov. 11:14), perhaps call a fast and pray, and get up under your Daddy's wings (see Ps. 91) until you can hear properly and move soberly. He will point you directly back to your Fiancé, the Word, and you *can trust* His instruction. He "is not man, that he should lie" (Num. 23:19), and He will *never* leave you or forsake you (see Heb. 13:5). His plans are to prosper you and not to harm you (see Jer. 29:11).

Every good and perfect gift comes from our Father (see James 1:17), and if a prospective mate doesn't see himself as a gift from God to your life, to serve you as God's daughter and as his sister in Christ, then he for sure won't see you as the gift that you are. Truth.

The vows we make tie us on a soul level. Numbers speaks of it. We have biblical examples of people who have vowed crazy things, and in the face of having to pony up, they did even crazier things to fulfill their obligation (see Judg. 11).

Ask Dad to show you by His Spirit any unhealthy vows that you have made, and repent (see Rev. 2:16). Renounce these things out loud. Confess, and receive your forgiveness and cleansing (see 1 John 1:9). Your enemy will throw up 216 reasons for you not to release those vows: he'll give you awesome visions of lonely nights; he'll throw two old single ladies in your path who are best friends at eighty to remind you that you can't trust your Dad to fulfill the desires of your heart; he may throw some kids your way to threaten that your ovaries are too old. He will use every tool of self (including self-help) to keep you tied to an ass (biblical word for donkey!) that is dragging you aimlessly through a field in which nothing can or will ever grow.

He will accuse you before your Father and say that you are not worthy to be released from the vow, the yoke that your soul is tied to. Rebuke him in the name of Jesus, turn the channel, hold your Fiancé's hand, say yes to Jesus (for some of us, again). Dust your cute little hiney off, and keep moving forward!

Unhitching Your Yoke

I remember a particular relationship to which I had made a vow in my heart and mind, even to my heavenly Dad. When the man said goodbye, I became the woman at the well, adorned by guilt and pain and in my gown of shame with a broken heart and torn clothing. Thankfully, Jesus met me and offered me His cup of salvation once again (see Ps. 116:13).

I could have argued as I had in the past that I wasn't worthy—selfdom again. Grrr. But this time I didn't.

I didn't run to my usual comforts: excessive first dates, flirting, becoming a super religious nun chick, ordering a lock for my chastity belt, beating myself up day and night with guilt, overeating, drinking, becoming social queen of the month or supermom of the year. I no longer had the strength for all that. I was spiritually, emotionally, and physically dehydrated, and *thirst* was birthed.

So I said, "Okay, Lord, my faithful Fiancé, I have *no* idea why You would still want *me* back, the wife of Hosea [see Hos. 1:2], but I'm here. I'm listening. I'm torn, broken, starving, dehydrated, and ready to receive Your water—as much as I can at a time." I said yes to my faithful, merciful, forgiving Fiancé, and now I sit here, with you, encouraging you that there is a robe of covering and a way out. I too have been blind, willful, stubborn, beguiled, naked, and left for dead. Raped by the enemy of my soul and my agreements with him.

Repent, sweet babies. Repent. "He is faithful and just to forgive us our sins, and to cleanse us from unrighteousness" (1 John 1:9). That's love. Love covers (see Gen. 3:21; 1 Pet. 4:8).

That's our Dad, and that's our Fiancé. They can and will, alongside you, disavow those agreements that you've made that have bound your soul to less-than-stellar choices, mistakes—sins. They are eager, hopeful, and willing to join you in your faith, even faith the size of a mustard seed (see Luke 17:6), so that the Word, your Fiancé, can move those mountains and bear fruit in your life (see Luke 8:8). The Word came to serve, and He still desires to serve us. (That was a sweet, life-altering revelation for me.) Jesus said that He came to save, and as the greatest, He is the servant of all (see John 13:12–17).

As I toiled over the fact that I was *still* betrothed to my Fiancé even after playing the harlot, my daughter said to me, and I quote, "Mom, you can be one man's bride and another man's whore." Ouch.

When it gets rough after unhitching our yoke, we will be tempted to revisit the tomb of our broken vows. Sometimes to lay flowers of tears and regret. Other times to curse through the stone, hoping that the corpse inside can somehow right the wrong agreements we made not just with them but with others from our past too. See, whatever we have not forgiven and (since our enemy plays so fair) even the ones we *have* forgiven will rise up to remind us in a fabulous display of self-pity that we are, in fact, forsaken. That we are forgotten. That we are old maids in the making. That somehow God can't be trusted because of the silly agreements we've made.

The good news? "He is a liar" (John 8:44).

Our Fiancé says, "Let the dead bury their dead" (Matt. 8:22). Amen? Take off your grave clothes, sister. They stink. They are wretched. We are not called to live a mournful life due to sin (see 2 Cor. 7:10) but to live an abundant one due to victory through the cross. We are called to sanity, which results from a fantastically safe and intimate relationship with our fab, faithful, and powerful Fiancé.

Fragrant

Cleansing is a giant message of our Dad's. (Be Berean—look up how many times the word "cleansing" is used in His Love Letter to us. It's major.) As women, we understand cleanliness. Even if only outwardly. Barring complete demonic manifestation in us or abject poverty, generally speaking we like to clean up and smell nice.

God loves a good aroma too. We see this in the Old Testament regarding the sacrifices offered and the pleasantness of the aroma that ascended into heaven. It's so cool that our Dad can smell! But before you spray that new Gucci fragrance (which I love), let's take a look at our Dad's favorite fragrance.

Our Fiancé's sacrifice was the ultimate aroma to our Dad (see Eph. 5:2), because Jesus was perfect and never fell short of our Dad's glory (see 2 Cor. 5:21). He represented Him fully in the earth. When He took on our sin on that cross, hanging there naked and bleeding, He gave His perfect blood. He became sin.

He drank vinegar and hyssop directly before His last breath (see Ps. 69:21). Hyssop was mixed the blood on the Passover doorposts; the blood was fragranced (see Exod. 12:22). It's interesting to note that when our Fiancé was first offered the vinegar and myrrh, which has an anesthetic quality and would have numbed His pain as He hung there in pain, He denied this numbing concoction and bore the full weight physically, emotionally, psychologically, and most importantly, spiritually, for the entire world. Wow. Just wow. Makes me wonder how many numbing agents we are offered on a daily basis that would keep us from taking up our daily crosses as His daughters. (See the addictions course again.)

Can you imagine sending your precious baby, your unstained child, into a brothel to be the subject of multiple atrocities stained with the sin of immorality that would end in a heinous death? As a mother, I can't. Not for anyone. But our heavenly Father sacrificed His Son for you and me, and our Fiancé agreed to it. Willingly. He was not murdered. He laid His life down for us (see John 10:18).

Since as women, we like to please, let's look at the aroma that is pleasing to our Fiancé: the man who is our Savior (Jesus was fully man and fully God). And without being woo-woo about it, let's look at what pleases our Fiancé. It's simple: "Jesus said unto him, Thou shalt love the Lord thy God with all thy heart, and with all thy soul, and with all thy mind" (Matt. 22:37). So whether you are in your sweats with no makeup or all made up, this is His perfume of choice: a life lived in remembrance and appreciation of what He gave for us—a life lived in truth, mercy, and righteousness. *That* is a pleasing aroma to the entire Godhead. Imagine.

Push

Sometimes living a life pleasing to our kingdom costs us everything. I mean, let's be real. We can recite and actually agree with the words on the page and sing hallelujah, but when it comes to being ostracized, alienated, rejected, wronged in every way, mocked, or threatened, our faith rises to ask for our decision. But never forget this: all heaven rises with you.

Push through. Our familiar comforts don't like to let go. They present themselves differently at times, but they still have the same agenda: to keep us stuck and living a half-baked life.

Every possible dating candidate from here to China has come out of the woodwork to ensure that I don't stay focused on finishing this leg of my race—the writing of this book. Every business opportunity or explosion has taken place as I wind down my efforts. My own father passed on to glory during this writing process. My daughter left for college. My life has virtually turned upside down. But I'm determined to finish this portion of my race, whether bloodied, bruised, or afraid. So yeah, I've had many reasons to turn back to familiar comforts.

When I recognized this temptation, the Lord sweetly took me to the passage about Jesus sanctifying Himself for His cause: others (see John 17:19). He set Himself apart and didn't fall prey to lower living, because He was here to redeem us.

I am not here to redeem you as He did, and if you sat with me in traffic on any given day, you would know that I'm not cured of lower-level livin'. But *I am* here to bring God glory by exercising the spiritual gifts that *He* blessed me with for the kingdom.

This has called me to lay aside a few things that are distractions for me. Dating is one. Worrying about my businesses is another. I'm finally at a place at which I think He's worth it, you're worth it, and so am I. Amen? (White hanky, please.)

Safety in a World Gone Mad

As I jog on to finish this book, the world around us seems to be falling apart, quite literally. Our country is in turmoil, our currency is being devalued by the day, Israel is at war, Islamic extremists are terrorizing the world, and our government is proving to be impotent due to incompetence and no accountability.

All this ignites some very real issues for me as a woman. Very simply, who will keep me safe? I mean, I'm not afraid to shoot my way through anything, but this runs deeper. While the question of my safety is a legitimate and honest one, I also know that the enemy wants to ensnare me in worry, fear, and drivenness concerning these issues.

I don't know about you, but trusting that God will care for me and protect me in times like these usually puts me in mind of another of my "lust list" items: powerful men. (It was revealed to me that the enemy has taken my idea of a powerful man and presented me with men in big-boy suits—outwardly powerful yet spiritually sporting proverbial pull-ups. Since I'm a mama and love to nurture, I end up in the fantastically exhausting position of savior, quasi wife, private investigator—and spiritually and emotionally buck naked.)

When I've agreed with the lie that I need a man to be safe, I've made decisions based on fear and on my own understanding, both of which serve nothing but the enemy's kingdom. I've been left with resentment, bitterness, guilt, anger, wrath, jealousy, fear, and accusation toward the *boy* and toward myself. Again, placing our trust and expectation in someone who has not been appointed to be entrusted with our heart is futile and unnecessary. Inevitably we end up separated from our heavenly Family, the Godhead, on a soul level that feels nothing short of a desert island in the pit of hell. But God (see Ps. 139:8). He is our refuge (see Ps. 91).

As I've said before, the only way that we will *ever* know who we are is to ask *Him*. A man will never show us that entirely, because he didn't knit us together in our mother's womb (see Ps. 139:13). Our parents, careers, friends, possessions, service will fall equally as short.

I do believe that a great marriage can nurture the greatness that Dad placed in us and show us many things about ourselves and spur on our working sanctification, as it were. But if we operate from the likeness of the one who caused the fall of man—the abusive father, Satan—and look to our men to be our cisterns when they are stagnate pools of sludge because they aren't going to their Dad and Savior either (1 Cor. 11:3), we will most assuredly fall short of the life we have been called to: love. For them and for ourselves.

Spend Time with Your True Love

If we truly knew (like when we *know* that we know that we know that a man loves us) how much we are loved, how solid the God-head is, how assured we can be of that truth beyond feelings and circumstance, then we would gladly and readily exchange all our despair, accusation (toward self, God, and others), impatience, envy and jealousy, covetousness, anxiety, drivenness—all our vows—for our Dad's promises. For His peace and quiet confidence (see Isa. 30:15). This level of being only happens when we spend time in fellowship *with* our Fiancé, the Word, and become practitioners of what He reveals to us.

This requires *our* effort. That may seem obvious, but you might be surprised how many people I minister to who have no idea what or how God thinks or feels on any given subject. It grieves me greatly. It is the leading cause of people's captivity. It seems that many are hoping that their pastors will feed them, but our pastors and priests are not our "holy spirit." They may usher us into God's pasture, but we have to feed on and develop from the pasture ourselves (see Isa. 55:6). The world may find it beneficial to blame-shift and subvert accountability, but our kingdom doesn't operate that way.

Our pastors and priests might make us stand up and shout for the hour or two we are in church. They may bring us to tears, inspire us to hang on just one more day and not lose hope, reprove us or instruct us, baptize and marry us. But I'm here to bear witness to you that they are *not* a substitute or even a remote comparison to the fellowship that is crucial and, more importantly, freely given to us by and through our Fiancé with the Godhead.

On the flipside, don't forget that the horizontal is as crucial as the vertical within the realm of sanctifying salvation—the two are not mutually exclusive. If you are hugging yoga mats in lieu of fellowship with the body, you err, my dear sister (see Heb. 10:25). (Not to mention that you are summoning and worshiping other deities.) I know that we can all get on each other's nerves, and we are a hurtful bunch at times, but God knew that when He placed fellowship in the order of life.

Fellowship and sanctifying salvation are one. It's in relationship that we are wounded, and it's in relationship that we are healed. (I am not saying that fellowship saves us. It sanctifies us—perfects us.) People are always God's number one agenda. Our Fiancé's sacrifice for us is proof.

As much as we ladies love to talk, one would think that earnest prayer time wouldn't be an issue for us, but I find that with most of my friends and acquaintances, prayer is merely a lifeline thrown out as a last resort or a religious duty in which one respectfully bows his or her head and says what's appropriate. (I've been there too. Ugh.)

Our heads may be bowed and our lips reciting the appropriate words, but God knows the inward parts, and He hears our hearts (see Luke 8:17). There is no hiding anything from our Dad because, well, He's God. Duh. Praying is the greatest tool we have for communication with Him. So what's the holdup?

Revelation 5:8 gives such a beautiful picture of where our prayers reside: our prayers are literally incense in gold bowls before the Father's throne. What?! That's awesome. Talk about treasuring words that someone has spoken. *Our Father treasures our prayers.*

Got Baggage? Bring It

It's time to get honest, ladies. Honest with ourselves. We need to bring all our trash, everything the enemy has "gifted" us with through our own life's circumstances and those of our generations, and boldly come to our Dad through our Fiancé, God's Love, Jesus (see Heb. 4:16), the One on the mercy seat, and say, "Okay, Dad, here I am, yuckies and all. Let's do this."

Now *that* is a heart He readily receives and cannot *wait* to hear from. Why? Because a broken and contrite heart is something He is close to (see Ps. 34:18). Why? Because He's our Dad, and He *is* love. That fact has *nothing* to do with *our* sins or *our* righteousness. We have no righteousness outside our Fiancé, remember? He said so (see Rom. 3:20–21).

While we are fundraising and feeding children on remote islands in the name of practicing our faith and pleasing God, let us not forget to bring all our guilt, shame, fear, restlessness, control, manipulation, deceit, ungodly gain, envy and jealousy, confusion, bitterness, blame, escapism, discontentment, drivenness, strife, striving, perversions, daydreams, hopelessness, depression, heaviness, addictions, and whatever vows are not of our Dad (bring that lust list you made) and cast them *all* upon *your* Fiancé (see Ps. 55:22; 1 Pet. 5:7). Then enter in through the narrow gate (see Matt. 7:13; John 10:9). This takes courage. This is faith.

If we don't, in spite of clothing the naked and feeding the hungry, we are living in disobedience—in other words, sin. How? Because we are refusing to do what He instructs us to do. Not caring for our own lives, we are clinging to vows that keep us separated from Him. Almost worse, we are fellowshipping with things other than Him (see 1 Cor. 10:20), and the objects of our vows are nothing more than repugnant slave drivers that offer an oasis we are ever chasing in the desert of our lives, only to leave us with a mirage!

We are not only listening to but living with sweet nothings and ignoring our Fiancé's sweet everythings. We are falling "short of the glory" (Rom. 3:23), because we are agreeing with the enemy, and we weren't created for his pleasure but for our Dad's (see Rev. 4:11). My ministry time with women reveals this—and my own life has reflected it.

We are trying to have a relationship with our Fiancé through others (the equivalent of asking another woman into our honeymoon suite), achievements, sin, our children, our jobs, and the world. But I'm telling you, while our Dad's mercy endureth forever, our Fiancé is like, "Hello? I've written this amazing Love Letter full of sweet everythings just for you. I've written this song, a serenade, *just for you*, because you are Mine and I am yours and I died for you.

I love you. You are engraved on My heart. You are a necessary part of My body, and I need you to nourish My body and be the jewel in My crown." This is as much personal as it is corporate.

As much as you are sighing and swooning over these love words, batting your eyelashes and finally relaxing your shoulders for the first time in months, some of you tuned in to a naggy little voice inside you saying, "Seriously? How am I someone's jewel?" (It speaks to you in first person.) When you heard it, instantly a recording of every indiscretion you have engaged in began to play in your mind. Every lie that has shaped you up to this point.

The father of lies and his lying kingdom are speaking to you. Yet the Word tells us that observing "lying vanities" causes us to forsake the very mercy available to us as His precious creation (Jon. 2:8). To observe something is to pay honor to it, the equivalent of observing a special holiday. Yuck.

The Word, our Fiancé, is our banner (see Exod. 17:15; Ps. 20). He is the standard for truth in our lives, because He *is the* truth. Any other voice, thought, feeling, impression, or imagination is vanity. It's that creepy guy we mentioned. Cast the creepy guys upon Him too! Our only hope in making it through this life with any real sanity—contentment, joy, safety, peace, and prosperity (not just money)—is in fellowship, in intimate time spent with our Fiancé, ogling as we look in His eyes and listening intently to what He has to say to us, for us. It's in hearing His heart toward us and for us.

If you are American, you understand what the U.S. flag means not only to you but to the world. The flag is our banner. It says to us, "We are united; we are strong; we will fight to the end, and we intend to have victory." Or it says to others, "Holy tamoly, the strongest nation on the planet is among us!" Men have sacrificed greatly so that our flag can fly as high as it does.

Jesus, in a far greater way, gave *all* so that His banner, His Word (Himself), would carry the same kind of weight in our lives while we are on this planet and beyond. The Word tells our enemy that he's about to get a whoopin'. When we appropriate it, that is. He's already defeated by our Savior, but do we know that and live it? I often say that it's dangerous not to know what we don't know. Ask Him to show you what His Word says and what it means for you.

Give ' Up

Our Fiancé tells us to ask our Dad for what we need (see John 16:23-27) in His name. In faith in Him and in what He's done for us. In His character, image, and likeness. I am reminded of the instance in which our Fiancé was praying to our Dad for what He wanted: He prayed that the cup of suffering would pass from Him (see Matt. 26:39). Much as we do, He asked several times, and in humility He ended His request, "Nevertheless, not My will but Yours be done."

This is what we need to do with our crazy and dangerous vows—tell Him what we want and then trust Him with the results. Can you, from your heart, request something and let it truly be His will that is done?

Your enemy knows you intimately. He knows your cravings, your lust list. He helped your generations craft that list, and he helps you keep it going, robbing the Ones he hates more than us— the Godhead. Think about that for just one minute: when we cling to our vows, not only are we being robbed, but our Father is being robbed of us, His precious creation.

But the things to which we make our vows are takers, draining us of our very lifeblood, our hope, and our joy in the name of what we think we want or need. Father knows best and is jealous *for* us (see Deut. 6:15). Our Fiancé deserves us. And according to our Dad, we deserved Him from the foundation of the world.

We were created to look and be just like Him. Lucifer, our enemy, had other plans (see Isa. 14:12–15) and has worked to steal us from our Dad for centuries. But Dad's mercy *endureth forever*.

Cleansing Your Palate

* Have you made any vows, spoken or unspoken? What are they?

* Which mountain have you circled several times?

* What is your idea of casting your cares upon Jesus?

* Can you think of any addictions you may struggle with? Again, drugs are not the only addiction. Bitterness and fear can be addictions too.

* Do you think that Jesus understands what you go through?

DIG A LITTLE DEEPER

Look up Genesis 3:15, Romans 8:15, and 2 Timothy 2:21, and share with your sisters or write down what each passage says about what happens when we serve the enemy and what happens when we serve God.

Speaking of Daddies, Who's Yours?

Ye have not received the spirit of bondage again to fear; but ye have received the Spirit of adoption, whereby we cry, Abba, Father.

ROMANS 8:15

If you ask ten women who their daddy is, most will, understandably, reply with their earthly father's name. I know some of you as Christian ladies are saying to yourselves, *Well, of course I know that God is my Father!* But I want to know, who's your *daddy*? Who is your heavenly Daddy to you?

This question is important, crucial, life-altering, and threatening. It's paramount. "Life threatening?" you ask. Well, if you don't know who your daddy is, you are basically OYO (on yo' own). And we are no match for our enemy and this world on our own (see 1 Pet. 5:8).

On the contrary, when you *do* know who your Daddy is, it is threatening to your enemy's kingdom. It's no wonder he enjoys our religious occlusion when we think of God as some bearded, unattainable, one-sided meanie in the sky.

See, thanks to our precious Fiancé, by our adoption we now call God Abba Father, Daddy. *Big* difference from being on our own (see Rom. 8:15).

Father or Daddy?

My sisters have always referred to our father as Daddy. I, on the other hand, quit calling him that when I was very young.

It always bothered me over the years that I just couldn't bring myself to utter the name "Daddy." Could not do it. I coveted my sisters' ability to say this word that meant so much to me but that I just couldn't say.

See, my relationship with my daddy began when I was two (I never knew my biological father). And this man who fell head over heels for my mother and me had three kids already, two girls and a boy, who were significantly older than me. My mother and I were not a welcome entity in their lives. Their world had been blown apart by an unforeseen divorce, and now, a few years later, here came a pretty German woman who couldn't wait to adopt their dad's Greek heritage and her little blonde snuggie who (at first) just wanted to cuddle with her new daddy most of the time.

My father adopted me as his own and gave me his name, and despite our challenges, our family went on to live a fairly peaceful existence. Still, it was fun not being wanted by your siblings and not understanding why. But my dad did the best he could. Yeah, the enemy was forging his kingdom when I was very young. But God.

In my young teen years, the enemy decided to manifest in our family, resulting in several pretty tumultuous years on planet earth together. My father, unlike our heavenly Father, was a human and could change (as all humans do). When he did, I could no longer *view* him as my daddy, much less call him that. My siblings could not relate, since their relationship with him was totally different than mine.

Because of this breach, God, my heavenly Father, wore the face of my dad. Even while singing about Him, reading about Him, and teaching about Him, deep down inside I had a human view of God working against me. It was only many years later that, in His mercy, He showed me that this is why I kept making the same agreements with the enemy, resulting in the same ridiculous choices in men and in my life in general.

It was simple: I didn't trust God, much less like Him. I wanted to, of course, and I thought I did, because I was a good, faithful daughter. It wasn't until God gave me a revelation about why the enemy had gotten into our family (more on that in a later course of this meal) that compassion and then forgiveness was aroused toward my precious earthly father, and I could actually believe that God is who says He is and call my dad Daddy again. My view had changed (see Matt 6:22). Priceless.

The Power of Adoption

But there's more to the story.

A few years back I was renewing my passport for travel outside the U.S. I couldn't find my birth certificate, so I contacted my state of birth for a copy. Finally, after a delay, I received a call from the records office of that state asking if I had ever gone by another last name.

See, I had put my birth name on the request. That had seemed like the obvious name my birth certificate would be under. However, what I learned next was pretty amazing.

Apparently, when a child is adopted, the name he or she was given at birth no longer exists. It is sealed and will not come up in a records search, ever. It's gone. Null and void. In turn, the adoptive father's name is placed on the actual live birth record. *As if he had been present at the child's birth.*

I hung up and cried. A lot. Not only was it a beautiful mental scene to think of the man who had chosen me as his adoptive daughter being present for my birth, but I was moved because in His mercy, God showed me very clearly the correlation between that earthly legal adoption and the heavenly legal transaction that took place through the blood sacrifice of our Fiancé (see Gen. 3:15).

Our names are no longer associated with our original after-the-fall birth father, Satan. We are as far from that relationship as the east is from the west; it is in the deepest part of the ocean (see Ps. 103:12). We are now sealed by God's Holy Spirit (see Eph. 1:13).

Because we have been adopted, bought back, according to our Love Letter (our Fiancé, the Word), God is now our Daddy again, and nothing Satan says can change that. We can, however, live ignorant to that fact, blind to it, willfully disobedient in it, but it *does not* change the fact that God is our Daddy and that He's calling us to accept it, trust it, know it, live like it, *be* what that agreement brings about.

In this relationship He has made every provision for us to crawl, sit up, waddle, stumble and fall, inquire, make mistakes, run ahead, fall behind.

He is wooing us, ladies. Right now. He is teaching us what a daughter looks like, what a Fiancé looks like, and what our enemy looks like. And guess what? *We* are *not* our enemy. Our enemy is our enemy! We are not bastard or orphaned children. Priceless.

Living in Our Father's House

In times past women frequently left their daddy's house and went straight to their husband's. Now we go from mom and dad to our college dorm or an apartment and spend several years without a husband. We work our way through the systematic jungle that we call our professions, hang out at happy hour, go to the gym, plan girl's outings, date online, involve ourselves with our church groups, do laundry, get our nails did (yes, I'm a beautiful mess).

Most of us spend time *single*, ladies. We worry, we get lonely, and we count wrinkles and pounds (it is what it is). We also dream and hope and wait. Or we convince ourselves and agree with the enemy of our soul that we don't need a man. We can make our own bank. We can buy our own car, take our own trips, dine in our own fine establishments, and buy our own bling.

We sing along with pop artists/gods on the radio about not needing a man and about how chicks somehow rule the world (remember that order thing?) and accept it all as life. And while there is *zero* wrong with having any of the above-mentioned blessings, the heart in which we attain them and keep them determines which kingdom we are in agreement with and who we answer to.

As singles, we also craft "the list." Not the lust list this time—you know what list I'm talking about. That all-in-the-name-of-Jesus list that no man will ever be able to live up to. Because, after all, we are God's princesses, and we deserve a man who will recognize and worship us. Seriously, ladies. We need a revelation and a dethroning.

But in the end many of us settle. Our list proves futile—and so does our faith. We curl up with the lies of the enemy while showing up to church to convince ourselves and others that we are still what we say we believe.

Some of us wake up in the morning, in all our nakedness, to a warm and sometimes unfamiliar body, and we try like crazy to run for the cover of every excuse, even the mercy that has been provided us in the name of "grace." We proclaim "God knows my heart" to the nearest shower, where we secretly hope that the stains left on our souls from last night's adventure will wash down the drain and that we can pull ourselves together long enough to seem okay as we remind ourselves of the last romantic comedy in which it really did work out for her and *they* became a *them* and lived happily ever after.

Yep. I'm outing us. Because I love us. And more importantly, our Fiancé loves us (see John 3:16). He has earned the right to speak to us in this personal level. He paid more for us than any earthly man ever could. He walked through hell for us (see 1 Pet. 3:19; 4:6) and stared our adversary in the face. Yeah, the one lying to us and luring us into beds defiled. The one numbing us with career ladders, being the best at everything, designer everythings, sex-toy parties, drunken nights, regret-filled mornings (concealed by pounds of makeup to hide the scars he inflicted on us and our generations). The one directing movies that tell us it's all gonna be okay—it worked out for J. Lo (my personal fave romantic comedy actress), so it can work out for us too (and sometimes it does, but not without a price).

Remember, ladies, as single women, not yet married (physically or spiritually), we are in our Father's house, belonging to our Dad. And it's important for us to remember that we were purchased with a heavy price. Heavy. As much as I love, protect, relish, feed on, and use words to paint intricate pictures for the soul, I'm not quite sure one could accurately put into words the depth and measure of what actually took place on that cross and subsequently in the heavenlies and on earth. I know I can't. Our redemption and adoption is truly a work of the Holy Spirit in the individual heart of man. Only God can draw us to Himself (see John 6:44; Acts 2:47), and only through the cross of Jesus, our Fiancé, the bound and perfect sacrifice, can His wooing be conveyed to the human heart.

Our Fiancé faced that created (see Job 1:6), defeated (see Isa. 14:12–17; Rev. 12:9–11) being, Satan, and snatched the keys of death (see Rev. 1:18) right out of his blood-soaked fingers and said, "*These are Mine!*" That, ladies, is our Fiancé, our Savior, our hero, our best friend, our brother, our healer, our Redeemer, our *everything*. He's the man who kicked every spiritual behind to save ours.

And that's good news, girls! He *is* the good news!

But the draw to the cross of Christ demands a response from us. What is yours?

Holy Hotties or Naughty Bodies?

In course 3 we touched on being the vessels of the Holy Spirit. I want to go a little further into your heart regarding this honor that we have. As God's adopted daughters, living in His house, engaged to His Son, we have a responsibility to keep our vessel pure.

My heart aches with the revelation that God is giving me concerning our earlier question, "Who's your daddy?" He's enlarging the eyes of my heart to see just how much not only my spirit means to Him but also my soul, my mind, and my *body* (He dwells there!). See, our soul will go on into eternity. It will continue to think and feel and perceive. That is a very sobering thought when it comes to the choices we make now (see Luke 16:19–31). Particularly regarding who and what we share our body with. It matters. It all matters.

We tend to view our spirit as some spooky separate entity in which all things holy take place, and it is, but guess where our spirit resides? Yes, in our *bodies* (see 1 Cor. 6:19). If we look at what happened when those not consecrated to touch the ark of covenant, which held the Spirit of the Lord, came near it, we might shudder in fear (see 2 Sam. 6:6–7). But we *really* need a revelation of this, ladies. A serious one. Anything unclean could not come near the ark, lest it be destroyed. It was super serious business. And guess who houses the Ark of the Covenant and who is God's temple now? *You* and *me*.

You and I *are* the house of His Spirit. That includes every part of you—body, mind, soul, and spirit. I always remind women and men that as much as we like to buy the lie that we girls can separate our private parts from our hearts, we can't. And if we do, God help us. (And He will. He did it for me.)

Defiling our vessels is not the unforgivable sin (see Mark 3:29). Let's clear that up—I am not interested in loading anyone down with guilt and condemnation. But I *am* interested in calling women into God's vibrant and necessary romance for each of us, His bride-to-be, to allow Him to cleanse us, purify us, and change us so that He can present us to Himself spotless, blameless, without wrinkle (see Eph. 5:27).

This happens by our Daddy's Spirit and prompting *and* by our obedience. No other way. It isn't spooky magic, and it requires our participation as does any successful, meaningful relationship. I'm not talking about earning our salvation, because we can't; I'm talking about walking out our salvation daily in reverence and appreciation (see Phil. 2:12).

We don't always skip through the tulips about this either, let's be sober about that. We can, but sometimes we just don't. Many factors, from our own hormones to our flesh to the prodding of our enemy, lend themselves to the ever-looming temptation to be cranky and out of sorts.

When my daughter gets cranky, I just let it be okay, because I know her heart when I tune into my Dad's Spirit about her. I love her right on through it, and she shakes it off quickly. She usually just needs a hug and no words. Just my presence. He longs to do that for us too. If I take offense at her, however, and leave my daughter to her grouchy attitude, I essentially abandon her on the battlefield. She is held captive, and we are out of fellowship.

I am called to protect her, love her, and comfort her, not accuse her in her moment of weakness. That is our Father's nature, and He uses our Fiancé, the Word, to comfort us by His Spirit if we would but go to Him, even and *especially* in our bad moments. Even in our doubt and unbelief (think Thomas; see John 20:24–29) and anger and hopelessness (and Peter; see Mark 14:66–72).

Living as His Daughters

We defraud our Fiancé, who died for us, and our Father, who adopted us, when we lie down in the name of sexual freedom (see 1 Cor. 6:19–20). Again, no condemnation; only love, ladies. Can you receive that?

If you can't, *please* ask our Dad to show you why. Don't sit there and ask yourself, because you and I don't know our own hearts. Contrary to popular "follow your heart" memes, the Word warns us that our hearts are deceitful (see Jer. 17:9–10) until God has illumined (see Heb. 4:13; 8:12) and washed them (see Eph. 5:26).

Don't ask your girlfriends either. They don't know what's in your heart, and if they are anything like mine, God love them, they will tell you how wonderful you are, that nothing is your fault, that it's normal and God understands. And He does! And you probably are wonderful, and it really isn't your "fault"—it's the sin that lives within you (see Rom. 7:17).

But *it is not normal* for blood-bought daughters of God, engaged to the King of the universe, to be bed hopping (see 2 Cor. 11:2) while proclaiming, "Boaz is coming!" It is not normal. It is the way of the world (see Gal. 5:19), and we were bought back from death (see 1 Cor. 6:20) and sin and the world.

We are "a peculiar people" (1 Pet. 2:9). We have what the world wants. We shine (see Matt. 5:14). We stand apart. We are savory (see Matt. 5:13). We are safe people. We are loving and loveable (see 1 Pet. 4:8). We are sanity (see 1 Cor. 2:16) in this crazy place. We are light in this darkness (see Matt. 5:14). We are a voice in the wilderness. Whether we feel like it or not, this is who we are. (Wavin' the white hanky. Can I get an amen?!)

We are the only visual the world has of our kingdom. We are pure. We are holy (see 1 Pet. 1:16) because of Him. We are alive. We are called to live, and *can* live (see Phil. 2:13), as such.

Turn. Confess (see 1 John 1:9). Repent (see Rev. 2:5). Receive and restore. He is faithful to finish the good work that He began in us (see Phil. 1:6). He needs us to say no to our cisterns, our whoring, our addictions, our vows and say yes to Him (see Ezek. 14:6)!

He will not trump our will, because He is loving. He will allow us to make agreements in the earth that are not of Him (see Ps. 81:12), yet *He* will *never* forsake *us* (see Deut. 31:6; Heb. 13:5). He will whisper to us (1 Kings 19:12), He will shout (Jon. 1:4), He will send others, but ultimately, it will be our choice to say yes. If it wasn't, we would have the equivalent of an arranged marriage.

Some of us are living as if this was the case, riding on the salvation coattails of our parents and grandmamas and no closer to knowing our Father or our Fiancé than the man on the moon.

Your salvation is just that: *yours*. Receive it, if you haven't already, and if you find yourself face to the face with the enemy telling you that you've lost your salvation and that he has it in his hand, rise up! Face that lie head on, get on your face, and cry out to your Father.

Your Fiancé will come to your rescue like you can't imagine. I don't care how stinky, naked, battered, and raped you are by the enemy of your soul and your agreements with him. Call on your

Daddy in the name of Jesus with your "faith as a grain of mustard seed" (Luke 17:6), and receive your life back, girl. We need you. And truth be told, the world needs you!

We don't own ourselves any more, ladies (see 1 Cor. 6:20). Our bodies are His. His temple. His holy habitation. Yes, *you* are holy ground. You are valuable real estate that the enemy would love to maintain lordship over, and he's a horrible landlord. I'm just telling you. He lets things leak, allows us to become infested with parasites of all kinds, tears down all our walls, and leaves us exposed for every manner of beast to come in and out (see Prov. 25:28–29). No offense, but if our Father entrusted the womb of a woman (see Luke 1:31) to house, nurture, and carry the life of our Lord and Savior into this earth, don't you think we owe it to our own wombs to keep them places of holiness? Selah.

Some things can't be washed away with a pill or with the next sit-com that makes light of worldly living. Apart from actual physical disease, there's nothing worse than the slow death of a soul meant for abundant life. And *He* determines what is abundant for us within holy parameters.

You *know* that you were created for more. Because you were. I was too, and I'm finally writing this book because I believe it, know it, and have said yes to it. I love you, and if I could wrap my arms around you right now with a giant warm blanket and hold you and let you cry it all out, I would. If I could put my hand on your heart and heal all those fractured places, the tiny fissures that leave varicose veins on our souls, I would. I can't do that—but He can. He wants to. He is calling you (see Rev. 3:20).

Saying Yes

If you have this book in your hand, you are being presented with the opportunity to make a decision, one that He will not require you to fulfill alone, but one that He has earned the right to ask you to make: will you say yes to our adoptive Father and to our Fiancé and live as Their daughter and bride-to-be?

You are not a ho, you are not a survivor, you are not a trick. You are not the ex, you are not an independent woman (as it were). You are not a hottie with a naughty body, you are not your PhD, you are not a sorority sister, you are not Ms. Goody-Goody, you are not your next handbag or fab shoe purchase, you are not a double D, you are not your next Botox appointment, you are not a super Christian, you are not super mom.

You *are* simply spectacular. A mystery that only He can unveil. You are a marvelous and fearfully crafted creation. You are holy. Stunning. Adorned with precious oil (see Matt. 25:4). You are His jewel. You are a valiant warrior. Who needs the Ya-Yas (I love that movie) when we are kingdom princess warriors? You are more than you now imagine. You *are* the weapon.

In our present-day culture of female worship, we need to be clear about the order of things. Don't misunderstand all I've been saying. We are not greater than our Master or our Brother (our Fiancé). We need a sober pill. Women were not called to the rule the world as the world proscribes.

I take exception to my fellow artists who develop mantras that infer otherwise. The bride-to-be taking charge is *not* of our Father's kingdom. Our Fiancé overcame the world's system (see John 16:33), and we are called to "occupy" the territory (Luke 19:13) until He returns. Then we are to reign as "kings and priests" (Rev. 1:6) unto Him, and all things flow from Him.

He is the head (see 1 Cor. 11:3), and that will never change. Contrary to my Greek counterparts' quote (I love *My Big Fat Greek Wedding* too), when it comes to Christ, the neck doesn't "turn the head." No, He is the mind from which all answers, concepts, and truth flow. And we have the mind of Christ (see 1 Cor. 2:16)! We need to study to show ourselves approved (see 2 Tim. 2:15), use His truth, and live.

Shelve the Dangerous Stuff

As you agree with your Father and say yes to your Fiancé, you may want to take some measures to protect your sweet time with Them.

For instance, when I quit smoking, I had to stop meeting my friends at the bar after work. Not because I had a drinking problem but because I had a *smoking* while drinking problem. When I drank, I smoked. When I was on a long phone call, I smoked; when I finished a meal, I smoked. There was a time when I just couldn't meet up with my friends for an after-work beverage or stay on long calls. Seriously. I had to protect my commitment to be smoke free.

In some seasons I chose to give up girly chick flicks that would tell me it was okay to bed hop because things all worked out in the end. I had to put Mr. Darcy away in the closet (he's like my emotional, dreamy crack pipe—not even kidding), because *Pride and Prejudice* lulled me into a drunkenness whose hangover I could not afford, since I was feeling lonely and forgotten by God where my own Mr. Darcy was concerned.

The only way for me to get and stay sober was to avoid the proverbial alcohol causing my drunkenness long enough for my Dad to honor my Fiancé in my life in order to heal some places, bring me through the temptation, and bring me to a new awareness and depth of His love for and understanding of me as a girl, a woman, a bride in waiting.

I had to submit my emotional and mental masturbation to crucifixion long enough for me to get to a place of healing, wholeness, understanding, and ultimately life. And make no mistake, I'm still on the road to recovery. The M word may disturb some of you, but it is what it is. Comforting ourselves in lieu of His comfort is not the way to life.

So if you have to order the granny panties to keep from showing your next date your new lacey undies and push-up set from Victoria's Secret, *pre-order them*. If you need a chastity belt, order it. If you need to shelve your girly chick flicks, lock 'em up. If you need to quit texting the latest pursuer drawing you to nowhere-but-bedville, cut him loose, girl. If you need to quit hanging with the recently divorced, "all men are rotten, and we have earned the right to destroy our lives through illicit sex and by secretly turning to women for comfort and understanding" (ahem) girlfriends, *cut 'em off*!

This is *your* life. *Your* salvation, *your* eternity, *your* sanity. As I tell my daughter, forget the dumb guy and move on! Take those cute little heels you prance around in on credit and that shiny new bag and all the weaves and foils and look to your heavenly Fam— your Father, your Fiancé, and the Holy Spirit—to find your soul. Remember, ladies, once again, how you get 'em is how you've gotta keep 'em. Protect your growth at all costs. *Not* in fear or zealous religion but in sobriety, with eyes wide open.

I have *no* idea what's in store for you and me, but it's better than what Hollywood could offer on its best romantic day. There's nothing stuffy or boring about our Dad, our Fiancé, and Their holiness. *Nothing*. (Song of Solomon comes to mind). You owe it to yourself, to Him, to your family (earthly and heavenly) to do the work to run to and in freedom.

Don't believe me? Do it and see for yourself—then send me the praise report. Your sisters need you.

Cleansing Your Palate

- Who is your father?

- Do you believe that he loves you? Why or why not?

- Has he told you that he loves you? How do you feel about the answer?

- Would you trust your father with every detail of your life? Why or why not?

- What do you believe about your body?

- Does shame play a role in your life? If so, in what way?

- Can you list any areas of your life that need to be cut off? If so, what are they?

DIG A LITTLE DEEPER

Look up Psalm 103:12, John 6:44, and Ephesians 1:13, and share with your sisters or write down what each passage says about the blessing of belonging to the Father.

Course 7

Survival Mode

Jesus answered and said unto her, Martha, Martha, thou art careful and troubled about many things: But one thing is needful.

LUKE 10:41-42

We love the show *Survivor*; it gets great ratings. But notice the yucky stuff that it takes to survive: backbiting, suspicion, division, fear, competition, comparison, envy, deception, cunningness, coveting—and all to win the luxuries of food or recognition. With that show we are basically tuning into Satan's family hour (see James 3:16) and calling it entertainment.

We weren't called to be survivors. The show's music is catchy, but the *world* survives. Animals survive. No disrespect to the ill who are proud to be alive because they survived. How about if God faithfully sustained them? When I think I'm surviving, the emphasis is on *me* and *my* ability to overcome something on my own.

I notice more and more of my girlfriends, myself included, filled with worry trying to care for everyone and everything and inevitably, ending each day in exhaustion (see Luke 10:38–42). Of every kind. This is *not* the abundant life our Fiancé charged us to live.

Ministering to women allows me to see this disease pattern in most of them, usually as a result of heaviness, a broken spirit, and heartbreak. They're trying to be something and someone they were never called to be.

I get it. I'm in this race with you, remember? (See Isaiah 58—we are moving through this meal of restoration together.)

The problem is, some of us think that we are not worth life more abundantly. We were not only birthed in but shaped by a survivor's mind-set. We learn skills of adaptation to our environment to obtain, sustain, and maintain a life built on sand (see Matt. 7:24–27).

There's more for us.

We've Been Had

Staring into the countless eyes that I've been entrusted with through ministry, I've come away with one realization: we girls are tired. Being a survivalist is hard work. We put on a brave show, and no one would ever know that, not so deep down, we ache. We are exhausted.

Age is not a variable.

Through our twenties, we learn how to work it. We pay homage to that expensive education and to our parents' dreams for us. Some finally close the deal on marriage, usually to someone everyone else thought was great (and so did we, at least for the moment). After all, we looked good together. We enjoyed each other. We laughed. We shared. We felt right. But somewhere along the line, whether through our husband's death or divorce (and from what I hear, the former is easier), or through separation or abuse or adultery, we woke up sore and fragmented.

In my younger years many of my friends made their living onstage, and here's the lie: everyone thinks he is in control—both the one throwing the cash and the one taking it! The client in all his glory has the power to decide the object's (naked woman's) worth. She has the power to make him want her while taking his cash (and probably his family's), and she meets her girlfriend later to talk about what a sucker he (and all men) are. But it's all a farce—everyone's been had. It's the world system at its finest. Equal-opportunity users and destroyers.

Yes, most of my dancer friends hated men. And truth be told, many of you do too. You can substitute the word "hate" for "strongly dislike," "lack respect for"—whatever shortage of love you prefer—but it's all the same. We either idolize men or hate them when they are based on a means to an end. And that too is birthed straight from the throne of hell (little t).

I remember when women couldn't even go to a pole bar without a male escort. Now we have female stars making it cool to "make it rain," and those who used to be our closet freak girls have now graduated to "Girls, Girls, Girls" night out. Sigh. We've been had. If you don't think this is happening to girls in our churches, you need to wake from your slumber.

Yep, I visited a few of these places too in my younger years. When you've been an object of desire most of your life, you survive (there's that dreaded word) by making *peace* with your demons. (Freud and his peaceable demons can take a hike.) You become a hostage while thinking that you're a survivor. The prostitute somehow thinks she's the pimp if she just changes her perception.

My *roaring* early *twenties* left me whimpering by thirty. But God.

Looking for Validation in All the Wrong Places

Our angst and heartbreak usually make their appearance physically first. Our minds become so separated from our hearts that our bodies are the only voice left crying in the wilderness of a life left to its own devices. Disease sets in to an otherwise toned and tanned body, tirelessly working to preserve an appearance that simply doesn't match up with the hidden parts of us.

If food is our comforter of choice, we end up with legs we thought we would never have and the shame of a waistline that reveals our secret misery. Either way, the heart is finally telling on itself by way of outward expression, saying to the world and to our own mirrors that we believed the songs we chant: "I'm every woman," and "I've got my own thing," and "Don't let 'em see you cry," even though "everything he owns is in a box to the left." (Although I never understood why any of us would want "another him in a minute." Again, catchy, but not what we, as His inheritance, are called to.)

What was once a battle cry, just a song we sang with astonishing agreement and fervor, has now turned in on us, the one it was supposed to sustain—alas, revealing what a lie *it* really was while pointing a finger at *us* for believing it (our enemy doesn't play nice). We were never created to rely on ourselves (see Prov. 3:5).

(As a recording artist and songwriter, by the way, I believe that Satan himself oversees the music industry. After all, he *was* music, the light bearer, praise [see Ezek. 28:13–14]. Look no further than a song not only to encourage but to validate our goofy decisions that we were never intended to live out. The proverbial quintessential abusive relationship: schizophrenia. Fragmentation at its finest.)

Our twinkle gone, we are in danger of fading into a lifeless, over-medicated, overworked ghost of a being meant for life and that more abundantly. And if we believe in a distant, impersonal god whose name is Universe, we're not only going to have trouble ever discovering who we are, but we will continue to look for validation and understanding of ourselves through every other medium in that universe.

Now I am an advocate for physical health and taking care of one's body. I believe that this is part of our responsibility and in-heritance, part of loving ourselves as we are commanded to do (see Mark 12:31) so that we can then love others. I'm not talking gym-rat activity (think balance), but a thoughtful regimen to care for one's temple is a great prescription for rejuvenation and overall physical and mental health.

Many of my counterparts, however, use exercise and other modalities as a form of worship. And trust this—some modalities are exactly that: worship of one god or another (poses don't lie).

I'm saying that the good news of Jesus is not only more than food and raiment but can't be substituted with yoga mats. Sadly, though, many in our faith make this replacement and call it a spiritual experience.

Baby, I love my Pilates class, but you can inhale and exhale slowly your way into hyperventilation and never find your way to "the peace of God, which passeth all understanding" (Phil. 4:7). A physical toke is a poor substitute for absolute freedom.

Dehydrated

I'm thinking that the reason we won't have oceans in the new earth (see Rev. 21:1) is because women have cried enough tears to house the world's sea life into eternity. "Beauty for ashes" (Isa. 61:3).

While we forge our way through life with a smile, bank parties, and cuteness, something in us knows that something isn't right. Something in us remembers what He whispered into our spirit before we emerged on the world scene: that *truth* that all the lies have worked like mad to help us forget.

The reason we accept the lie and the role of shouldering our own burdens and the burdens of the world while proclaiming to be satisfied in Jesus is because so few encouraged us to stay at the well to complete our meal and quench our thirst (Matt. 5:6; 6:11). (I mean, who wants to be associated with the woman at the well? Remember those vows we denounced earlier?)

Let's face it, most of us don't even know that we're dehydrated. Scientific studies show that, physically speaking, the majority of people are *chronically* dehydrated.

I'm here to suggest that hydration begins on the spirit level—and a great many of us are parched. Our pharmacists could tell our stories, and if not, our alcohol, cosmetic, and apparel sales-people certainly could. Don't get me wrong, I like all these things—wine was the first miracle, I run a cosmetics business, and I'm the president of an apparel line. But these sweet additions to our lives become a comforting carrot, sugarcoated with that ever-luring lie that if we are in control, we can't be hurt. It keeps us neatly fastened to the hamster wheel in our stilettos. But God.

Yes, diseases prominent in women tell the story of our nakedness or our heaviness or our starvation. They strongly point to the fact that we have believed the debilitating lie that we are somehow in charge of it all—and that if we're not, we could or should be.

When Our House Crumbles

The world with all its seduction has nothing new to offer (see Eccles. 1:9). It is not selling freedom. It's selling us—short.

The world either wants to worship us (Gen. 3:6) or blame us for its problems, and from our wounded hearts, we finally agree that it should be so (Gen. 3:6, 12). In turn, we step out of our order in the creation of things and are left coveting everyone else's life and *things* until we reach a place at which we are drained of all hope.

We will never be the women He has destined us to be without first knowing who He says we are individually. (Have you heard that in every chapter so far?) If we put on the glasses of comparison during this process of discovering who and whose we are, we run the risk of staying stuck in survivor mode and drivenness and self-everything: hatred, bitterness, rejection, or pride—which is really fear that we aren't enough and that if anyone, including us, ever discovered that, we would crumble and die.

But the crumbling of our houses built upon the sand (see Matt. 7:24–27) of achievements, careers, acquaintances, children, husbands, boyfriends, church involvement is the best place to start finding out who we truly are.

When our childhood dreams are occluded to the point of what I call "hope deferred dementia" (see Prov. 13:12), we may finally collapse at the feet of our beloved Father and simply exhale.

While many are showing up at His feet through a myriad of modalities, these are not His idea of intimacy (see John 14:6). See,

God honors His *Word*, our Fiancé (Ps. 138:2), above *all* things and watches over it and is careful "to perform it" (Jer. 1:12). If we have no Word, we have nothing for God to watch over to perform or to honor above all things.

Now hear me clearly, He is a patient Dad and looooooong-suffering—I'm living proof. But what we need is a meal called Jesus. Not an esoteric experience for the soul. We don't need a mirror to try to figure *ourselves* out to fix *ourselves* (see Prov. 3:5–6). Nor is it true that if men would just get right, all our woes would end (although . . . jk).

It's *Jesus*, the Word, who can and will meet your heart's cry, wherever you are (see Ps. 139:8). In *Him*, our Fiancé, is newness of life, mind, soul, body, and spirit (see John 3:3; 2 Tim. 1:7). If you're crying out for Jesus, get ready for the most filling meal of your life. You'll breathe easier, because *He* is your very breath (see Gen. 2:7).

Draw Near to the Word

So what does the Word tell us? What does our Fiancé's have to say about our survivor mentality?

First seek ye "the kingdom of God, and his righteousness; and all these *things* shall be added unto you" (Matt. 6:33). Our Love is telling us that our Dad already knows what we need. We don't have to sustain ourselves. We can lay down our burdens and let Him take care of us.

Remember, I am a wordsmith. I prepare and eat words for a living, for sustenance, for understanding and to be understood. I *love* words. So semantics are something I weigh carefully. In the case of my Fiancé and His words, I try not to give heed to semantics and take His Word for exactly what He says. He doesn't ask us to read between the lines. He knows exactly how to reach each of us individually within the structure of our personal struggles, obstacles, triumphs, hopes, and dreams, with the same truth.

Our Love Letter is not open to individual interpretation (see 2 Pet. 1:20). The Word speaks for itself. In a multitude of counsel, however, there is safety. So if I have a question about something I read in the Word or am teetering on woo-woo thinking or believing, I ask my elders. My pastors, my covering.

The enemy knows the Word better than we do. Remember, he's so vain that he recited the Word back *to the Word* while tempting Him in the desert (see Matt. 4:1–11). (If it wasn't so insane, it would almost be funny.) Thankfully, Jesus didn't "survive" in the desert. He lived by the bread of the Word (see Matt. 4:4), and He used the Word to answer the enemy and defeat him.

My apparel tagline states, "Satan hates you," and for obvious reasons adds "Duh" (don't underestimate him). He knows you, your weaknesses, how you think and process, what you want to feel, and what you think you need, and he uses those fleshy things, those soul things, to draw you into woo-woo thinking or to get you to believe that you need some weird experience regarding the Word or to make you think that the Bible is too hard to understand or that someone else knows it better than you because they are more special or chosen.

All hogwash, as older Southern women say. Pure hogwash. Lies. Don't believe those things. The One who created you (see Col. 1:16), the One waiting to marry you, knows exactly how to speak to you through our eternal, breathing, never-changing Love Letter. "We have the mind of Christ" (1 Cor. 2:16) (present progressive—ongoing action), so we are obviously equipped to understand our Father. Duh.

Jesus took many opportunities throughout His ministry to get alone with His Father and commune with Him in prayer. We need to do the same, His Word open in front of us. We draw nigh to Him, He draws nigh to us (see James 4:8). Amen?

Life Abundant

Let's be clear—you don't have to be forty (as I was) to reach an a-ha moment.

If you are a young reader, let this message serve you (see John 13:8). Let your elders serve you. We'll chat about female relationships more in another course of this meal, but I want to stop right here and say to my younger readers, on behalf of your older sisters, that I apologize, take responsibility for, and repent to you as a fellow woman for not teaching you and loving you by celebrating you and your stage of life. We abandoned you to the world's system by agreeing with the enemy: comparing ourselves with your youth in envy, jealousy, fear, and worse, joining the world in idolizing your stage of life to the detriment of us both. Titus 2:3–5 comes to mind as a recipe for proper order of relationship and culture.

I *love* young people! I am extremely young at heart. (I have my mother to thank for that. She would rather hang with a group of forty-year-olds than with those her age.) Speaking of the elderly (my mom is rightfully considered an elder), I *love* them too. We all have so much to glean from each other (see 1 Tim. 5:1–2).

And I love being fortyish, although I truly wish that I had known in my twenties what I know now. I am no longer a survivor, adapting to the world and fighting to sustain my life. I am happy in my own skin, and even better, I'm grateful for the heart that He is continually birthing in me as His daughter. I'm a grateful woman with the wonder of a child.

The enemy of life has stolen a lot from me (see John 10:10) as a woman, but as the Godhead restores the years that the locust has eaten (see Joel 2:25), I have the opportunity to fall deeper and deeper in love with my Fiancé. Finally I have someone to hold onto who has never betrayed me, abandoned me, or reminded me of my failures. Instead, through them He brings me back to life (see Ps. 103:12; Rom. 8:28). And He will do it for you too.

We folk *in the middle ages* have some (as my former pastor calls them) "issues for tissues"! If you are a younger woman, pray for us. Do *us* a favor and love us instead of judging our mistakes or our desperate attempts to hold onto the stage that you are blessed with right now. Love us in Spirit and in truth. Don't give up on us or avoid us. And even in our busyness and our failures, remind us that you need us and we need you.

Survivors tend to go it alone. I think of being dropped in the middle of nowhere (which I've always thought would be a very cool weekend thing to do) and making decisions about direction, food choices and rationing, and where to camp *on my own*. But we aren't called to do that in everyday life. It's dangerous. Our equal-opportunity enemy speaks to all of us all the time to rob us of our relationships in any given stage of life. Don't let him.

Can our Father see us through when we choose to go the survivor route? Sure. But He wants life more abundant for us. He wants us to overcome. There's only one way to practice that, and that's with and through our Fiancé and in fellowship with His people.

Cleansing Your Palate

- What is your definition of a survivor?

- Do you believe that you are a survivor?

- What are you carrying on your shoulders today? Who or what causes you to carry that burden?

- What are your spiritual gifts (not talents)?

- How do you feel around younger people and older people?

- Are you invested in another female's life? If so, who, and how are you invested? If not, who can you invest in?

DIG A LITTLE DEEPER

Look up Proverbs 3:5–6, Isaiah 61:3, and Luke 10:41–42, and share with your sisters or write down what each passage says about what God wants to give those who lean on Him.

Exposing Sweet Little Lies

I fear, lest by any means, as the serpent beguiled Eve through his subtilty,
so your minds should be corrupted from the simplicity that is in Christ.

2 C O R I N T H I A N S   1 1 : 3

In the summation of our faith walk, it basically comes down to this: are we living lies or truth?

Some years ago, when I was still killing the ozone with Aqua Net, a popular song, "Little Lies," emerged from one of my favorite groups. The truth about little lies is that there are none. They're all big, and they have consequences.

And they're subtle.

My daughter came to me one day with a moral dilemma. A friend of hers had asked her to copy a CD so she wouldn't have to purchase one. Since I am a recording artist, my daughter was all too familiar with the fact that CD downloads are a musician's paycheck. But she was about to justify stealing by playing the Robin Hood card: she didn't care for the person who had produced the CD, because he was not exactly godly, and she therefore felt that it might not be wrong!

How many times have we thought things like *that*?! (God probably has a new book with my name on it titled *Monica's 101 Excuses for Sin*. I'm just sayin'.)

I extended the sobriety pill that my daughter needed in order to make her own decision, her own agreement with *her* Fiancé, based on truth. Yes, she already knew that stealing was a sin, but I reminded her that the enemy lies to himself and those who serve him, and I told her that he was lying to her about this so-called martyrdom, which was actually pirating (see Prov. 12:19; Rev. 21:8). She got the point: *he* was the creepy guy whispering to her.

Think about that: Satan lies to himself, obviously (see Isa. 14:13), to his minions (see Rev. 12:4), and especially to those of us claiming to be God's (see 2 Cor. 11:3)! He effectively does this by cleverly communicating to us through our thoughts, feelings, beliefs, and ignorance, not to mention through other people.

My Own Big Lies—and My A-ha Moment

At the end of a recent week-long program that my previous home church offered, my eyes, mind, and heart were opened by our awesome Father in such a life-altering way that it set the stage for the completion of this meal. This is the key that set this captive free and unlocked my own prison door of not fully trusting that God is who He says He is.

I mean, I *believed* that He is who He says He is, but I didn't *know* it. I had the faith of a mustard seed to believe that He would forgive, protect, provide, have mercy, show up—all that God stuff— but I didn't *know* it. And I didn't live it.

Our facilitator asked us one simple question: "What is it that keeps you from trusting your Father?" That straightforward question began the loosening of a tightly woven knot of lies that I had believed my entire life about my earthly father, men in general, and for sure God.

My revelation was this: somewhere in my head and heart, I had bought the lie that my earthly father was helpless. Remember, in my early teens the enemy had gotten into my family and created havoc, and my dad had gone for me from being my Daddy to my father. Because I became the defender of the family and simultaneously the scapegoat, I took on my dad's stuff. I bore his burdens of generational guilt and anger and familial alienation and didn't want him to suffer from them. I thought that I could somehow protect him.

While my dad continued to provide for us as far as food, shelter, and clothing, the events that transpired in my family signaled to me in *giant Vegas lights* that this man I called Dad needed my help to be okay. And that bred in me a lack of trust toward others. It also bred in me contempt and an "I am woman, hear me roar" mentality. I've often laughed that I would make the most faithful hostage (I was an excellent co-dependent with a classic case of Stockholm syndrome), but the sadness behind that statement is that I did so. Until now.

I was held hostage for years by little lies that wove their way around my mind and heart and led me to behavior consistent with living lies. I was the quintessential faithful codependent friend, girlfriend, daughter, employee, and yes, even mother (we *can* be codependent with our children). I allowed the needs (or what I perceived to be the needs) of everyone around me to dictate my life and sense of worth.

Here's my favorite definition of codependency: my former pastor, Dr. Henry Wright, says that it's "calling that which is evil good—in the name of love." I *love* that, because it takes the psychoanalysis out of it and calls it what it really is. Let that sink in. I mean *really* sink in. Then think of any relationships in which you may be fostering this type of unhealthy bond(age). Doing this made me a rescuer. That's a place of power, in one sense, but it's out of order and exhausting. But *He is* merciful.

Since on some unspoken level I believed that my earthly father was helpless and virtually impotent when it came to certain areas of life, when it came to faith and to waiting for God in my own life, whether for a husband, a job, or healing, I grew weary. The years of attending everyone else's weddings and watching friends have more babies and seeing my own daughter bear an illness, my career at a stalemate as I nursed her, everything seemed so hopeless as it related to this all-knowing, powerful, I-know-the-plans-I-have-for-you, loving God.

I tried to help Him. I tried to *be* good. All the things I tried to *do* (the same things I had done to help my earthly father) to somehow prove to myself that my faith wasn't in vain led me to resentment, anger, frustration, and a half-baked belief that at the time I had no idea was operating. All this was fueled by the lies that I had believed about my earthly father and also my heavenly one. The enemy's architects are quite strategic in what they place on our paths to ensure a stronghold in our lives (see Eph. 6:12). But God.

When the program facilitator asked us what kept us from trusting our Father, I had such a sudden revelation of the lie that I had believed for so many years that I jumped up to the microphone and exclaimed, "*Wow*! No wonder I've thought God sucked all these years!" Yes. I. did. In all my transparent Monica honesty, under the burden of all the religious stuff I had been trying to "do" in the name of faith, I jumped for joy, publicly.

And I watched as others were then set free. Much to my surprise, my honest teen-like outburst resulted in roaring laughter, and people felt released to admit their own bag of yuck that they had believed about our Father. What had begun as a series of comments about our earthly fathers quickly turned for me into a major a-ha moment of seeing a direct correlation between my dad and his earthly weaknesses (which all men have) and my heavenly Daddy.

I'm not sure why we don't believe that Dad already knows what we are thinking and believing. He sees and knows all. So exclaiming my long-held beliefs about Him (which had been secret even to me) was not a shocker to Him. Amen? Romans 8:28 is definitely my friend: "We know that all things work together for good to them that love God, to them who are the called according to his purpose." (And 8-28 is my daughter's birthday, so this is a verse I can remember the address to!)

I gotta tell ya, the freedom I've finally gained has enabled me to sit here and share in these pages what I've wanted to express for years. During the years when my sin was evident, even as a believer, and kept coming back up as the same mountain, my remedy wasn't in place. Not really. In theory and belief, sure, but this was different. Now I was free.

When you know that you know something, it's just different. You can weather a lot when you know something or someone, because it is then that you can actually live 1 Corinthians 13, otherwise known as *love*.

Some of the things we struggle with are not a matter of our doing, per se. There's a reason we are told that generational curses have been broken by our Fiancé (see Gal. 3:13). We don't know most of our genealogy, but truly, all we have to do is look around, and we'll see some of the same-ol', same-ol' sin issues that are in our family in ourselves.

If Dad always worried about money, and we lay awake at night with dancing visions of poverty or how to clobber our workplace competitor to ensure our financial safety, well, samey-samey, sister. Generational.

If Mom had a hard time keeping her skirt on and choosing good men, we may see that coming down our lineage. If not with us personally, we can look around in our family—it's there. Abraham had a lying spirit, and that was transferred to several generations of lying based on fear of man (see Gen. 20:2; 26:7). I'm not taking away from his greatness as our elder, just pointing out historical facts that still attempt to plague us today when Jesus' blood is not appropriated in our lives. I'm not advocating that we just chant, "I plead the blood of Jesus." Appropriating His blood means recognizing our sins and our generations' sins that are still operating, even after Jesus' death and resurrection *and* our rebirth, and going to our Father's grace (the divine influence on the human heart) to get that stuff under our feet where it belongs so that we can keep moving toward *freedom*.

Replacing the Lies with Truth

So what turned the light on for me that day and exposed the lie I had believed for so many that my heavenly Dad was helpless? Well, for me it was reading and believing a particular version of the Bible whose wording conveyed to me a sweet little lie. And it kept me in major bondage for eight years of my Christian life. *Eight years.* Because of the sleight of *one word.* My life had been rocked and ruled by guilt, condemnation, and mercilessness from a God who, two verses over, was said to love me. It had all seemed a bit bipolar.

But now I saw it: Therefore if any man be in Christ, he is a new creature: old things are passed away; behold, all things *are become new*" (2 Cor. 5:17). Not "*became* new"—as in when I first got saved, and that was the end of the change in me. No, it was "*are become* new"—present progressive, ongoing action. A major light turned on. I was a continuing work in progress! God was *still working* on me! *He had not given up on me—and I wasn't to give up either!* I wasn't stuck in my ongoing struggles or my tendency to fail. I had every reason to hope that God was continuing to make me new, day by day. Wow. Amazing transformation right there.

As I have said often in our meal, "But God." When we include God in our lives and our generations and align ourselves with His Word, guess what begins to manifest? His Word. That's not to say that some areas of our lives in which these little lies have taken root aren't keeping His Word from manifesting fully, but we can rest in knowing for sure that as we draw near to Him, He *will* draw near to us (see James 4:8), and His Word will be honored and glorified. His Word is alive, as is Jesus. They are not mutually exclusive.

I've seen this. I'm a witness. My life is a testimony to *His* faithfulness. The only way to know if we are believing a little lie is to know the truth. Period. We have no other measuring stick in this thing called life.

Many voices cry out to us (see 1 Cor. 14:10), but I promise you, as someone who has listened to many of them, that there is only one truth—the Word of God. I had to reconcile myself to that in order to move forward with Him and in my faith. I've even broken this down to the version of truth that I will study (for me it's the KJV) so as to receive a well-rounded, nourishing meal coupled with fresh, no-added-minerals, living water.

We have many versions of the Word. Some of them are good, but others have not translated the Scriptures faithfully. For example, one version has eradicated Lucifer from Scripture entirely. I could list several problems with this (besides the fact that to do this one must take liberties that are swiftly warned against in those very Scriptures). When Lucifer is removed from the Word, then who was it, exactly, who fell from heaven, tempted us in the garden, and still accuses us day and night? Who was it that Jesus bought us back from? Who and what, exactly, are we saved from, if this being is so apparently disposable? Ourselves?

Yeah. GMOs are harmful to our health, and so is humanly modified truth.

When I finally realized that I had been beguiled through the enemy's twisting of the truth, my chains dropped away, and I ran with my backside on fire to a merciful, loving God of seventy-times-seven chances (see Matt. 18:21–22). Even then, the otherwise pretty, intricate, gold chain that I had woven had only one loosed knot, but it began the loosening of many others. It started with *God is not helpless* and moved to men are not helpless and we are not helpless. That was a game changer for me, honey.

We could focus on all the other little lies that the father of lies and people and life tell us—we are too this, or not enough that, or she has this, or you would be complete if you just had that, or her kids obey and ours don't, blah, blah, blah—but the deal is, if it isn't settled in our heart who our Daddy is and who we are to Him as

He created us from the beginning, how will we know who we are as reconciled, washed, redeemed daughters? *Nothing* we ever receive in life will make up for knowing this. Not even a husband.

We have to replace the lies with truth, or things and people become the replacements. When a relationship becomes the fruit of believing a little lie, it leaves us with a bitter stomach, and this is the seat of our spirit man. Not a good place to be.

So, my single sisters, settle once and for all the truth of whose and who you *are* and who *He* is. Draw near to Him, and He will draw near to you. Ask Him to show you those little lies in your life and even in your generations that have woven themselves into the fabric of your being, personality, and life. Exchange the lies for His truth about you, others, and, most importantly, *Him*.

The De-Frag of a Heart Hardened

Claiming this Christian faith of mine is one thing; living it is quite another.

The lie about the helplessness of my father and my Father is not the only one that dogged me for many years. Having suffered attacks on my sexuality in my younger years (see the appetizer at the beginning of this book, aka the introduction), something joined me during those terrifying, victimizing moments and whispered to me that somehow what was happening must be my fault. Another lie.

Everything became my fault. I look back now at people who whispered about me and came up with stories about me and my sexuality, and I wonder, *Did they see the residue of my perpetrators and assign it to me as my own guilt?* Either way, their accusations wounded me and eventually shaped me. But God.

It's dangerous being held responsible for others' joy, happiness, and understanding, not to mention their anger and suffering and sexual lust. It's a breeding ground for codependency 101. This is truly something that only evil could orchestrate and execute (see Eph. 6:12).

Because of this "lofty" position that others bestowed upon me, I eventually rebelled. Survivor 101. My give-a-ripper ran out about what others thought or felt about any of my decisions.

This showed up in my wardrobe.

Some say that women dress to impress other women, but my motives are quite the contrary. I could not possibly care less what women *or* men think of my attire from a fashionably acceptable standpoint. I simply dress for myself. I style my hair and choose my clothing according to my feelings, my mood, my beliefs about myself on any given day. *My* canvas. I grew tired of giving *people* that level of authority in my life. If I like it, I wear it. That can be a good thing, but it can also prove sometimes to be, well, contrary to Abba's opinion.

One morning I experienced a Spirit-birthed, through-my-Fiancé, changing-my-life-from-the-inside-out moment (see 2 Cor. 3:18). As I scoured my newly arranged closet, my eyes landed on a super cute little denim skirt (little being the operative word). I settled on a pair of tights and threw on my skirt.

As cute as I thought I was, I was immediately checked in my spirit. Something didn't feel quite right. I tried to ignore it and continued getting ready. Even threw on a longer sweater to make up for the lack of fabric in my skirt, ha!

Making my way downstairs for coffee, a Scripture dropped into my spirit: "Let every man be fully persuaded in his own mind" (Rom. 14:5).

This gentle tugging on my mind continued, and alas, I made my way to my Fiancé, the Word, to inquire of my Dad exactly what He was attempting to converse with me about. Lo and behold, I saw that Romans 14 and part of 15 addressed my miniskirt dilemma.

Yes, hard to believe that Dad would care about our attire. After all, a spirit of religion has freely used the Word, our Fiancé, as a weapon by reminding us in a hellfire-and-brimstone kinda way that the kingdom of heaven is more than raiment. Indeed it is, but the context of that is our Fiancé trying to get us to see the futility of *worrying* about and for such things (see Matt. 6:25).

But the spirit of what we wear and how *does* hold every bit of His attention. And why? Because it's all about love—loving Him, ourselves, and others (see Luke 10:27). Simple. He was the first One to cover us in our nakedness. And He still does (see Gen. 3:21; 1 Pet. 4:8). If we could only do that for each other (see Gal. 6:1–2).

So I read Romans 14–15, which specifically addresses food and drink, but then I landed on verse 7 of chapter 14: "None of us liveth to himself, and no man dieth to himself." Suddenly all bets were off, and so was my skirt! Therein lay my decision—I had to change clothes. I could have said, "Well, that was for then, and this is now," but love is love, whether two thousand years ago or today. I heard my Dad's heart through the sweet words of my Fiancé, the Word. Still, although I knew in my knower that He was speaking directly to me, I didn't exactly jump for joy skipping to my closet to change skirts.

No, I actually resembled my teenage daughter when she runs down the stairs with something that makes me go "ahem" and, with her head down and every grumble and justification in the world, she slinks back up the stairs to change. I take those opportunities to remind her that I've asked her to reconsider her attire not out of shame or a need to shoulder the burdens of someone else's potential struggles with lust or unholy, fear-based judgment but out of respect for her own body, which is His temple, and out of love for others.

I refuse to let Satan get a foothold of shame in her life just because he had successfully done so in mine through the lies I had believed. God is good. Communicating with her much as *He* did with me regarding my own cute little skirt is what relationship and trust is built on. Nothing religious or legalistic about that. At all. Nothin' but love.

Once the nudging subsided and the Word was deposited, I actually thought of the women I would encounter that particular morning and what their opinion could be. *Now* I knew that God was at work! After all, I was headed to a women's Bible study, professing to be a minister of the gospel, and I could hear some of the accusing voices already.

I'm a bit of the "Harper Valley PTA" type. My daughter can attest to this. People talk about me whether I'm wearing a body burlap sack or showing cleavage galore. It's never mattered. I learned moons ago to just do me, Monica.

Only problem with that is that because I dealt with so much rejection through my formative years, and I had basically quit caring what anyone thought, I could look the Christian "good girl" part by rote while missing the key component to this new Christian life: love.

Does wearing a miniskirt or showing cleavage mean that I'm going to hell? Uh, no. But it does mean that although in my faith I have freedom extraordinaire, as Romans 14 expresses, to eat meat, not observe manmade traditions, and so on, if I am going to walk in complete freedom and love, I simply don't place a stumbling block in the path of another who is weaker in faith. And let's face it, ladies, cleavage and short skirts can be a bit of stumbling block for most men with eyeballs, and we know it (but I'm keeping my yoga pants, even though I don't do yoga).

Again, this doesn't make us responsible for Satan's lies. A rape victim's skirt being short does not justify her being raped (that wasn't my attacker's motivation). Watching what we wear is about representing love and respect for our Father, our Fiancé, our brothers in Christ—and ourselves.

Now depending on how much of *myself* I'm living for in that comfy seat of selfdom, some days it's easy, and on others not so much. But if we say we love God but don't love others by soberly observing and honoring their level of faith with the freedom we have in Christ, then we are not walking the talk. Simple.

We represent an unseen kingdom in the earth. How we show up matters. Not in wardrobe only but in heart and mind.

God is forming a new, soft thing in my heart where hardness had formed, because the real issue is that I'd been hurt by humans and the enemy's resulting lies, and I had subsequently elevated myself by deciding to wear what I wanted, when I wanted, and how I wanted. If left unchecked, that would have (and *has*) crept into other places of my life in which *He* longs to reign as Lord, in love.

Jesus being my everyday Lord is very different from Him being my eternal Savior. After all, eternity seems so far off. In the simplicity of my mind, it's easy to think of Jesus as someone I will eventually experience one day, but as we've covered throughout our meal, that line of thinking and living is indicative of the lesser meal. Eternity is now—the ultimate present progressive.

As for the wardrobe thing, I often say that I would've made a great Eve. If I could live in a bikini every day, I would. (Maybe one day I will, docked in the caldera of Santorini.) Perhaps that stems from my European lineage. Something I love about my relatives? They aren't crusty or lusty about nakedness. Especially my German relatives. Are you kidding me? They're stuffy about most things, excellent about all things, and they will rock a blinding Speedo in a New York minute on a south Florida beach. Hilarious.

But modesty certainly has its place. Our Dad and Fiancé think so (see 1 Tim. 2:9–10). That's because They know what entered the world through our fabulously crafty and perverted enemy. In the beginning 101: people were naked. Then Satan (see Gen. 3:7).

Again, this issue of clothing is not about heaven or hell, as in salvation, but it's about *being* a daughter, not just *behaving* as one. It's about being in fellowship with our Dad who cares for us, right down to how we present ourselves in this world. It matters. It all matters. Not in some legalistic, religious kind of way but in love. (Now if He ever asked me to give up my heels, I may need a come-to-Jesus meeting.) We can be fashionably sassy *and* modest and still rock it. Amen?

As for our sisters who live in areas of the world with wardrobe laws that others of us simply can't fathom (*thank God*), the same spirit applies to laws of the land (see Rom. 13:1). If the law of the land says that heads are covered, well, then heads are covered. Now hear me clearly: every cell in my blood-bought, freedom-fighter, thanks-be-to-Jesus body rises up to shout, "Forget it! Jesus died for my freedom, and that includes being able to live freely with my head uncovered! In my country men and women died for my freedom to dress freely." But my reborn spirit, through my faith in Jesus the Christ, says, "Manmade laws can add nothing to me or take anything away from me as a redeemed daughter of the Most High God." Impossible.

Even some of the church seeks to rule with religious law. (We should first learn about spiritual covering before ordering our bonnets. Seriously.) However, when we live in divisive disputes over these things, it grieves our heavenly Father and Savior (see Gal. 5:15). While I may struggle with rebellion at times, one thing I seek to respect and understand is authority (see Matt. 8:9).

Customs of the earth do not affect the authenticity or freedom of the kingdom of God, because it is God's kingdom. Duh. I do not subscribe to any faith but my own—I think I've made that abundantly clear—but I know enough about my own faith to know that man's attempts to rule the world by the letter of the law and by misguided ideological theology cannot nor ever will usurp the freedom that I have in Christ Jesus on the spirit level (see 2 Cor. 3:6).

Little by little He is bringing me out of lies and into the fullness of His truth.

It's All About Love

Speaking of today's dreaded "four-letter" word, "authority" . . .

Having come from a home church that serves people from all over the globe, from all walks of life and all religions, regarding the correlation between physical disease and spiritual roots (see Deut. 28), on any given week we might have had any number of people in our service who dealt with various struggles (again, Eph. 6:12). Some of those were sexual in nature.

But I gotta tell ya, when I first began serving there, it was everything I could do not to fall into rebellion about wardrobe. I was so fed up with feeling responsible for others' spiritual issues, and because I had been a victim to this in my younger years, it all came back to haunt and taunt me.

By *His* grace and desire to change my heart toward those who had victimized me, one decision at a time, by agreeing with His truth (that is, submitting in obedience), I am breaking through (see James 4:7). But while serving in ministry, I realized that I had some fragmentation going on.

See, while on our church campus (which was in the boondocks), I dressed one way; and then I'd go back to the big city and my artistic life and dress another.

Now fashion sense varies, but in terms of skirt length, a little cleavage action here or there (I'm not exactly a size A, so it's a labor of love to reign the girls in), I didn't dare dress "that way" among my church, the elders, and the others we were serving. I mean, I was raised a Southern lady and all (cue woman fanning herself with a long Southern drawl). That being said, it became evident to me that I was playing a part. We are good at that, right? And because that's just what one did as a good Christian and definitely as a minister, I did it. But *privately* I wore what I wanted.

Even though through our ministry I was learning that all addictions, including sex and porn, are rooted in a need to be loved, when I was on campus with people who might be struggling, I felt stifled and oppressed by man's sin issues and what I perceived to be rules and regulations in this thing called Christianity. It was still about *me*, because my abusers had made it about me so many years before.

While I could *act* my way through my faith, I began to realize in my heart, not just in my head, that I had a choice not to. Not to mention, doing so was exhausting.

And honestly, I don't do fake well, so even in my efforts to behave well at church, I was in suspect-wardrobe land with my church elders. If I have a heart issue, I'm gonna wear it, quite literally. I was still subconsciously (on a heart and spirit level) incredibly mad about what had happened to me in my youth and the victimization that had stolen so much of my trust—my trust in God, in all mankind, and, sadly, in myself.

Because others used my body to fulfill our enemy's nature in the earth (to steal, kill, and destroy), I took my body back. (The next time you are tempted to judge the girl or grown woman dressed all wrong, check yourself—unless she's in white spandex. Kidding. But not really.) But in doing so, I *couldn't* and eventually *wouldn't* give up the reigns of this matter, even to a loving and personable God—a God who loved not only me, the one who was overcoming the victimization of evil, but also those who had agreed with it.

It's been rough. He's been patient. I was set up to take my body back in rebellion disguised as liberation in the name of *my* womanhood, not realizing that I had been liberated from the foundations of the world and that clothing had nothing to do with my freedom. In the end, what I wore was my inner self manifesting outwardly. As it always does. It was about love. It's always about love (see Rom. 13:10).

Through my time learning to love others and hate our enemy and live in the truth of God's Word, our Dad showed me through our Fiancé that our faith is, in fact, not about what we wear or what we eat but about our heart toward Him, ourselves, and others (see Rom. 14:7). This is what matters more than all creation to Him. Because the Godhead loves us, has hope for us, and needs us. (Yes, I said *needs* us—not to survive, but think about it—why else would our Fiancé have died for us? He has made us His hands, feet, eyes, mouth—we are His workmanship to fulfill His work on this earth and shine His light to others. This is the heart of His love story with us.)

Cleansing Your Palate

- If I told you that I loved you, would you believe me?

- If God told you that He loves you, would you believe Him?

- If I told you that Satan hates you, would you believe me?

- What is your definition of freedom?

- What is your idea of modesty?

- Whom do you really dress for?

DIG A LITTLE DEEPER

Look up Romans 8:28, 2 Corinthians 11:3, and Ephesians 6:12, and share with your sisters or write down what each passage says about the dangers of following the enemy's ways and the blessings of following God's ways.

Course 9

Between Us Girlz

God setteth the solitary in families.

PSALM 68:6

While many of us are busy walking for tatas and storming the world in pink ribbons, I wanna take a second as we wrap up our meal and talk about the importance of right relationship with each other as women.

For some of us, as I mentioned in an earlier course, the ugly beast of jealousy has robbed us of vital female relationships. But when mistrust sets in, before we know it, we have the war of the ovaries that literally results in sickness of our tatas (look it up). We are an estrogen-*dominant* society these days.

(For many of us, this is a generational curse. Someone somewhere in our generations proved to be equally as prone to the enemy as we are, and he or she did or said something that led us into captivity with them. Uh, yeah [see Num. 14:18; Prov. 26:2]. Again, yes, we are free from these curses, but are we *appropriating that blood* and living in victory over them?)

We ladies need each other. In our vertical relationship with our Dad and our Fiancé and the Holy Spirit, we can't forget our need for the horizontal. Going it alone will only hinder us.

Married Chicks

I can't tell you what a blessing it is to have women friends, especially married female friends, even as a single chick. Some of my friends have healthy marriages and some of them not-so-healthy ones. We can glean from both. If married women *really* knew how awesome it is for us single chicks to be included in family settings, they probably wouldn't believe it.

However, as a widow particularly, some women are afraid of having me around for too long. They fear that the husband will somehow want to save the damsel in distress. (Truth be told, if I'm not aware of my parameters and of proper fellowship, it could very well happen—and has.)

But God dealt with me on the sanctity of marriage many moons ago (another book!). It is my place to know my place, as it were, and to know that my friends' husbands are not my saviors or middle-of-the-night repair guys or friendly ears. As women, we *know* when something's up with a friend's boyfriend or husband, and we should respond according to love—love for our sisters and for their commitment or marriage.

Depending on the yuck still lurking in us (and others), it's a fact that we singles aren't always *safe* for couples to hang with. And sometimes couples aren't safe for us either, depending on their stuff. Seriously. But this isn't the end of the world. Just recognize it, go to Dad, seek counsel from your Fiancé, let Him heal you and give you discernment on the matter, and then get back in fellowship with whom He provides (see Ps. 68:6).

Don't let the jealousy of others or your own bought lies keep you on the outskirts of healthy relationships with your married sisters. When we isolate ourselves, we get into dating trouble—I promise. The strays of life find their way to our door for feeding and watering, and before we know it, they're peeing on our bathroom floors, hogging the remote, eating all our food, and worst of all, robbing us of our dignity, love, and, most importantly, our birthright. Ouch.

Likeminded Peeps

As for us and our single-friend choices, it's paramount to hang out with likeminded peeps. I'm just gonna tell you. I don't care how holy you think you are, our Fiancé tells us that bad company corrupts good manners (see 1 Cor. 15:33).

So, Miss Manners—"I would *never* do *that* or be like *her*"—just remember this warning. Much like missionary dating, missionary friending is exhausting and dangerous. I've heard it said by Harvard Business School professors that we are the average of the five people we hang out with most. Do the math.

Oh, missionary friending is great for keeping that self-righteous, in-control, "gonna save the world for Jesus by being best friends with it" lie in place, but I promise you that, as sure as I'm typing these words, His Word *will* be made manifest in due time (again, see 1 Cor. 15:33). Your good manners *will* be corrupted. I'm not saying that we should disown people because of where they are, but we need to know where their heart, head, and mouth are and with that knowledge make a spiritually educated, sober (not emotional or hormonal) decision about our place in their lives and how often we are in fellowship with them. If *you* are changing because of someone's company, it's time for a change of venue.

What does light have to do with darkness (see 2 Cor. 6:14)? (Yep, I was gonna be the sober barfly that represented Jesus to all the lost ones. Problem is, the little lie that I could save the world led me to becoming a regular in an environment that took advantage of the fact that I appreciate that wine was the first miracle.)

Girls "get" girls. We just do. I was never raised to trust girls, and I chose to be a guys' girl. I'm soooo grateful that Dad has changed my mind and heart regarding my species by showing me the wounds inflicted, lies bought into, ideologies subscribed to. And through repentance He has brought me to really cool friends, honest places of safety where I can express my desires, dreams, questions, and insecurities. Places of acceptance and trust.

Having girlfriends who pray for me as their sister is a new level of fellowship for me. Oh, we have our squabbles and little fleshy moments, but when we *do* what our Fiancé tells us to and address things in honesty and forgiveness, we rock on.

Not Always Easy But Definitely Worth It

I still struggle at times with comparison, particularly when someone doesn't have the same stains as me. But this enemy seeks only to rob me, again, of a valuable resource of fellowship, growth, and love. I am reminded that we all have our stuff, and that helps me rest.

I also find that it's hard to accept in others what we don't or can't accept about ourselves, and I'm here to tell you, our Fiancé is the only One who can heal those places. We *are* "accepted in the beloved" (Eph. 1:6). Period. (If I could add one thought to Ecclesiastes, it would be to be careful about who offends you. I have always found it true that whomever I am tempted to take offense with is usually a great source of blessing. Remember that the next time you are tempted to be offended or petty.)

If we look to friends to be our "holy spirit," this tactic will fail epically. Some friends will embrace this role, because they love being the spiritual counselor to everyone. But others will run because they see a need in us that they can't fulfill, leaving us feeling rejected and abandoned on the battlefield of life because they forgot to point us back to our heavenly Family, the Godhead.

I encourage you too, whether you are a teen or an older chick, to get yourself in fellowship with someone whom you can pour *into* as a sister. If you have stains, share them to help another *not* go down that road. And share your *testimony*—your *Fiancé's* testimony of faithfulness about how He brought you out.

When we refuse to share our past because of shame, we selfishly rob God of the glory, testimony, and hope that He wants to give others. We can leave the shame that the enemy drapes us with at the cross and be clothed again at the mercy seat. Get up. Shake that thing off (great song), and get to your mercy, baby! Arms are open. "His mercy *endureth—for ever*" (Ps. 106:1). He will wash you, change you, provide safety for you and give you a place of rest and restoration. Refreshing. You will be fresh, because in *Him* we *are* fresh (see Heb. 10:10).

Waiting for Our Fiancé

I think that as girls, we are wired to nurture, and the enemy attempts to pervert that by placing us in wrong relationships, whether with male or females. I am seeing in my daughter's generation a very scary numbing to the nurturing side of being a girl. Perhaps the sins of fathers (and mothers) of being driven, rebellious, and self-seeking are coming to roost now in this generation, but I see a real disdain for softness and even for tears. We've replaced love-making with *sex* for *every freaking thing* we see. It makes me batty!

Sex. The very word is sterile. Scientific. The "do it" word. That begs the question, what exactly are we "doing"? Many girls and women don't know *who* they're doing, much less *what*.

According to our Fiancé, when we have sex with someone, we are *knowing* that person. Joining to him. Becoming *one* with him. Him, his stuff, and the stuff of everyone else he's been with—physically and spiritually. And when we do this out of order (outside marriage), we are yoking ourselves with someone and lying about the emotional, psychological, and spiritual effects of it. The physical effects speak for themselves. Our bodies and hearts make deals with the devil that he knows we can't keep. But God.

By robbing of us of our very identity as Daddy's girls, the great liar singlehandedly ushers in perversions (in the name of experimentation), although they are nothing new (see Rom. 1:26). These addictions threaten to take us to places culturally where we honestly don't want to go. Not to mention their eternal ramifications. Yeah.

I'm not going to go into detail about sex, though, for one reason. I am sensitive to the fact that some of you sharing this meal with me have not traveled this road, and I don't want to stir anything before its time. (And this isn't that kind of book! I'm a poet at heart. If I tried to write romance, it would probably end up being a Christian version of a schmoozy novel that would leave some of you breathless. I'll leave that up to one of my favorite authors, Francine Rivers.) Even discussing the softness and true intent of our Dad regarding this thing the world calls sex can stir things for some of us and leave us daydreaming in Song of Solomon a little too long. You know I'm tellin' the truth. Especially for someone who hasn't known a man.

For those of us who have known a man (or several), we could actually use a new mind and heart regarding this whole sex thing. I think the fruit of our "labor" and the agreements we've made with our enemy speak to that.

But first we must start with *knowing* who we are, who our Dad is, and who our Fiancé is—the One who has asked for our hand in eternal life, beginning in *this* one. Stains and all. It is my hope that when we know who and whose we are, our hearts will be prepared to receive what *He* gives us and not what we take in lust, self-idolatry, and faithlessness or what we settle for because of a "clock." (Sarah had a clock—and now we have ISIS. Check out Genesis 16:1–12.)

I know that's easy for me to say—I have a child. And I can't imagine the frustration and fear that whispers to my single sisters who would love nothing more than to have children who don't (yet) have them. But in the waiting we can foster contentment and live a full life. We can overcome the resentment and frustration that tries to creep in. In getting to know our Fiancé and ourselves, our mind is renewed, our heart leaps, our hopes are restored, our purpose is ignited, our stains are washed, and our joy is returned. Life is more abundant.

For those of you who want children, your ovaries can rest, your milk can remain in waiting, and you can be free to live abundantly in joy, contentment, and excitement. Get involved with others' children through volunteer work or other means. Do you know how many children are literally dying a slow soul death because no one will pour into them? You don't have to be perfected to be a human being and just show up. Trust me.

I'm not saying that because we have said yes to Jesus, our lives are somehow saturated in perfect harmony and contentment. I am offering what I've found, and I have to practice living it daily.

We are told to labor to enter into our rest (see Heb. 4:11), and some days it is indeed labor. Childbirth was easier, it seems, but rest is our birthright. It's our love nest. It's our place to be groomed and dressed and ministered to. A place to be filled with that precious oil that we are reminded keeps our lamps burning. Let us be the wise virgins in this race (see Matt. 25:1–13). Let us eat from His banquet feast in the Word and prepare ourselves for that fateful night when our time in eternity is consummated.

We are *not* alone, we are *not* abandoned. We *are* loved. We *can* do this. He's counting on us, and all the kingdom is cheering us on.

Rest as a beautiful daughter of the King and bride-to-be of God's greatest gift.

Jesus may be all you've got, but truth be told, He's truly all you need.

Cleansing Your Palate

- Can you think of any female with whom you are not at peace (past or present)?

- Are you at peace with yourself?

- How do you feel around other women?

- What is your definition of sex?

DIG A LITTLE DEEPER

Look up Psalm 68:6, 1 Corinthians 15:33, and 2 Corinthians 6:14, and share with your sisters or write down what each passage says about the kind of company we should keep.

Dessert

Celebrate!

Congratulations! You've reached the end of our meal together. Give yourself a round of applause for making it here. No, really—put the book down and give yourself a round of applause! You will discover something super amazing if you actually do it. Ready? Go!

Okay, assuming that you actually followed the instructions to literally applaud yourself and celebrate your accomplishment and commitment in a real and tangible way, I'd like to know, how did it feel? How did you feel applauding *yourself*? If you felt great about it, well, that's awesome! The truth is, for most of us, applauding ourselves feels awkward, embarrassing, and somewhat contrived.

You Are Awesome!

I recently attended a well-known female televangelist's conference. As the leader rallied the crowd with statements we all know and believe like, "God is good! Amen?!" and "He has a plan for your life! Amen?!" the crowd went wild with applause. Then with the same enthusiasm she exclaimed, "*You* are awesome! Amen?!" Um, well, let's just say "cue the crickets" was in order. The silence was so palpable that I turned to my friend; we couldn't believe our ears. It *grieved* me greatly. I almost felt like a heel for applauding myself, but I had weathered too many devils to attend this conference, and mama wasn't gonna miss her opportunity to applaud *that*.

Somehow Satan has fooled many of us into *believing* that we are trash. I don't know how else to say it, because I honestly think that after my years of ministering to others and looking in my own mirror and judging myself with self-unforgiveness, this kind of thinking really is trash, and it must stink like it to our Dad and Fiancé. Seriously.

The dunghill. I've pitched a tent there for years, and apparently most of the thousands of conference attendees were camped out at dunghill village too. To make it all worse, we've got the devil lyin' to us and many in the church swearin' to his opinion (Southern folk talk). I liken this to one of my all-time pet peeves (aside from wet socks): floral bathroom air freshener. Yep, sprayed-over stink. That *wrong*, error-filled, religious-zealot teaching that we are scum. Albeit in Christ, but scum nevertheless. *What*?!

Considering the silence of thousands of Christians in that giant arena, I would say that this teaching is alive and well, whether it comes from our personal conversations with the enemy, from our pulpits, or from silence in our generations. Sadly, we secretly believe the age-old farce of a belief system that much of the church preaches and attempts to build a kingdom on: that we are just worms and that even *with* Jesus we remain as such.

Lord have mercy. Really. Like, *Lord, have mercy*, for they *know* not *Him* or what they teach. This is crazy theology and, frankly, teaching that gets my undies twisted like nothing else. Why? Because the enemy worked most of my life to make me believe that I was junk. Used goods.

He's right in that he did, in fact, use me through others' actions and eventually taught me how to use myself for his purposes. *But God*. Beauty for ashes, baby, beauty for ashes (see Isa. 61:3). The Redeemer.

See, when you've been debased by those who were supposed to protect you, love you, cover and honor you by honoring God's

Word in and for your life, you learn to either agree with the crazy teaching mentioned above or you work like a madwoman to debunk those people's words over your life. Yes, even as Christians.

Even as I've written this book, I have been nailed by the enemy with accusations of unworthiness. What's a girl to do in her flesh but what she's always done to survive (we've already covered this survivor mess)? Yep, hit the self button: self-exaltation, self-pity, self-comfort, self-debasement, and self-religion. Overcoming is a challenge. And not celebrating yourself is a sin just like any of the self-sins I just mentioned.

I mean, really, our enemy will stop at nothing to keep us tied up and twisted, and he will use our Fiancé, the Word, to do it!

The Joy of the Lord Is Our Strength

But God once again swooped down *with* His Word and other edifying believers to remind me and provoke my spirit that I matter. And so do *you*. And because of both those facts, I needed to get over *myself* and the enemy's usual tactics and keep moving forward to share His heart (and mine) to and for you.

It is *crucial* for us to celebrate with our heavenly Fam about who we are in Christ Jesus. Why? Because the *joy* of the Lord is our *strength* (see Neh. 8:10). When we celebrate our victories through Christ and our *choice* to say yes to Him and to our Father, *all* heaven rejoices (see Luke 15:7). Hello? And we should too.

I mean, *every* decision we make that agrees with Him matters. Many of us get stuck looking at our sin. We don't acknowledge, confess, repent, receive—and move on. No, we hang out next to Satan as he replays our failure over and over, and we never receive the joy of our restoration! If people knew how joy-filled repentance is, it wouldn't be such a downer of a message!

Think about how happy you would be if, when you had turned (repented) to walk another path, you could look back and see the bridge that you had been about to cross dangling from a thread and in flames! You would be *happy* that you had escaped destruction, and you would be *strengthened*, because our Father would be elated—and *His joy is our strength*. He will honor every single step we take away from sin and death.

Can you imagine how happy we would be all day long if we just walked around in perpetual celebration mode? The gospel is called the *good news*, people, and we are representatives and ambassadors of this good news! Do people see you coming and think, *Oh, here comes so and so with that floral air freshener she wears to cover up her stink. Praise Jesus!* or *Wow! Here she comes with Jesus again, and I want someone to love me and want me like that too!* Which one are you?

When my daughter was a baby, anytime she sat up, crawled, walked, held her own bottle, or talked, anyone near me would have thought that she had just landed the presidency. That is how our heavenly Fam feels about us! They are hosting a heavenly blowout, and if we don't *know* that, we will be down here, skipping through thorns, spraying air freshener over the yuck of the enemy. And *we* are *not* yuck. But we've already covered that.

Have you noticed that most people can't take compliments? My personal favorite is, "Well, praise the Lord, it's not me, just all Jesus." Yawn.

That has truth to it: apart from Jesus, we can do nothing. Jesus said so (see John 15:5). But we can discern the difference between false humility and appreciatively celebrating! When we say yes to what He asks us to do—to live, breathe, move and have our being in *Him* (see Acts 17:28)—*He rejoices*. And if we are seated in heavenly places in Him, and He's in us (see Eph. 2:6), we should be rejoicing too!

My former home church has a teaching called "Eight Rs to Freedom."[1] While reading this one day, the Lord lovingly pointed out to me that I was skipping one of the major Rs: *rejoicing*. He then gently showed me that overlooking this is the equivalent of someone throwing a party in my honor and me *not showing up*!

Celebrate with Him!

My daughter made the principal's list in her senior year at the Christian school she attended. In honor of the achievement of the students who had made the list, the school hosted a luncheon. My daughter's peers prepared the room with balloons and decorations, and the school provided pizza and other goodies. I know the effort that went into making the luncheon special because I was there the morning of the event for parents' prayer, and we were encouraged to vacate the room so that the kids could decorate for the upcoming gathering.

A few days later, as we drove home after school, with great enthusiasm I asked my daughter how her luncheon had gone. "Oh, I didn't go," she replied. "They were having pizza, and we wanted something different. So we went out to lunch." Stop. Insert Madea moment.

Some kind of Holy Ghost-righteous-indignation-meets-Regan-from-the-exorcist arose in me, and I exclaimed, "*What*?! You *didn't attend* your own celebration because you thought the lunch selection was *boring*?!" OMGoodness. I was temporarily nuts. I was so grieved on a number of levels that it manifested in anger.

Once I finished with my eyes rolling back in my head, my nails extending, and my nostrils flaring while telling her how spoiled these little "jerks" were (told ya, it was not a sanctified moment), I composed myself, and we got to the heart of the matter.

My grief over the fact that my daughter had thought so little of her own achievements and of others' desires to celebrate *with* her over them required us to have a come-to-Jesus moment. She had worked so hard for her grades and made commitments that had resulted in an achievement worthy of celebration, yet she had agreed with the enemy by not honoring those who had planned the party and herself and had just poo-pooed the whole thing.

Deafening silence fell over the car; you could have cut it with a plastic knife (probably like one they had used at the pizza party, ha). She didn't know how to reply. For my part, I felt like a whacko for having responded so crazily. I knew in my knower that this was a true defining moment for her, and I didn't want my reaction to trump the lesson. Still, the sun went down on my anger. *But God.*

The next day my daughter had a college fair to attend, and I didn't want her attending with confidence waning from the night before. Yes, as parents, we have the power to weaken our kids' confidence, because many times we forget that we are representing to our kids either the enemy or our Dad (see Eph. 6:4). She had made it this far and worked for this moment, and she deserved to attend the fair with her best foot forward and a twinkle in her eye. I wasn't going to let the enemy use unfinished business between us to stand in the way of her next celebration: the college of her choice.

So prior to the fair I repented to her for my tone and for my accusation that she and her smart, college-prep friends were little jerks. I reminded her of what an amazing young lady she was and how incredibly blessed I was by and with her. Whether she'd made a selfish decision or not, I still accepted her and loved her (see James 5:16). I did *not*, however, repent for the meat of what I had said the day before and the importance of the matter to her salvation (not as in whether she'd go to heaven or hell but as in whether she was bringing glory to her Dad or to the beast in her sanctification process).

She sincerely apologized to me and with a soft, contrite voice, hung her head down and said, "Mom, I'm sorry. I just didn't know." While Satan was busy preparing my guest list to the worst-parent-of-the-year party, I realized right then how many lessons this whole exchange had offered, right down to the two of us repenting for falling short of His glory. It was healing for both of us.

And that's how we roll in our house. We are honest, crazy sometimes, but we remember the Word. And we do what it says. When we forget, *He* reminds us, and then we do it (see Matt. 18:22). That's the only way we will ever *know* the man, our Savior, the gift of God at the well, much less ourselves: by being "doers of the word, and not hearers only" (James 1:22).

She apologized to her principal for the lack of respect shown to those who had planned the celebration, and she now *knows* the importance of celebrating her achievements. She *knows* who wove her together in my womb, creating that awesome brain of hers, and who gave her the ability to hunker down and make excellent grades, because I've told her. I've shown her, hung it on her neck, and put it on my lips: the Scriptures, His Word, the truth (see Prov. 6:21). It's not just on our walls in the way of Christian art. It is in her heart and mine, and when she missed the mark, I was able to stand in the gap for her, with her Father and Fiancé, and correct her. And because she has an obedient heart and a teachable spirit, she received it in love.

She now *knows* that in celebrating herself she glorifies Him and that by not celebrating herself she glorifies her enemy. We overcome the enemy "by the blood of the Lamb, and by the word of [our] testimony" (Rev. 12:11). That's awesome and something to celebrate!

Put on Your Dancing Shoes

The *joy* of our salvation is crucial. And while it is, in fact, all about Jesus, let us not forget that He died for *us*. Hello? He celebrates with us! We are preparing for the marriage supper of the Lamb, and that is not gonna be some stab-yourself-in-the-arm-with-a-plastic-spork-to-get-a-little-excitement kind of party. No, it's going to be the mother of all dinner parties. We are invited, and this life is preparation for it and for eternal living. Yes, living.

I know that, personally, I'm not pumped about inviting buzz-kills to my parties. Are you a kingdom-party buzzkill? The enemy would love to ride in on our backs to the marriage supper of the Lamb, like a Southern cockroach in the summer (I hate those things). God plainly states who is coming and who is not. All those who model characteristics of the enemy's nature are not invited—and not celebrating ourselves is his character. I don't mean that we're supposed to think we're all that. The enemy exalts in pride; God's babies, rather, say thank You to our Father in gratitude.

Put away your order forms for your robe, halo, and banjo pic. We've got work to do, people! We will rule and reign as kings and priests on earth (see Rev. 1:6). And *this life* is our training ground. God loves a good party, and He loves celebrating His children. Do you think that He is sitting in heaven with a sourpuss, grumpy-God face about life? (Now, *that's* a funny visual.) *No!* He's rockin' it when we rock it and comforting and cleansing us when we aren't (see 1 John 1:9). He is *for us* (see Isa. 41:10).

So put on your dancing shoes, get a candle with a cupcake, do a Holy Ghost jig, run a bubble bath—whatever—and shout a joyful noise every single time you rock it with a godly decision. Celebrate *every single inch* you take back from the enemy. Not in pride but in *gratitude*. You are saved, you are magnificent, you are worthy, you are honorable—worth every drop of blood that our Fiancé sacrificed for you. Own it, live it, rock it. We need you.

Celebrate your Father, your Fiancé, and yourself, and pass it on! Our greatest achievement is believing that He is who He says He is and that we are who He says we are—and then thinking, feeling, and doing what pleases Him. Believing and living from this place is practicing (doing) His Word, and that pleases Him, which is what we were created for (see Rev. 4:11).

Some days the fact that our eyes have opened to see another day is enough to put a smile on His face. You matter. Everything matters.

Rock on, single ladies! I love you.

Cleansing Your Palate

- If someone threw a party in your honor, how would you feel?

- If someone gifted you with both tangible and intangible rewards every time you did something according to their standard, how would you feel?

- Are you proud to say your name?

- What is your greatest achievement?

- What would God say that your greatest achievement is?

- Do you believe that God celebrates you? That God is proud of you?

DIG A LITTLE DEEPER

Look up Nehemiah 8:10, Isaiah 61:3, and Revelation 19:6–8, and share with your sisters or write down what each passage says about how God wants us to celebrate, and why.

After-Dinner Cordial

Let's face it, the distinguishing lifeblood that every culture is birthed and centered in can be found in cuisine. As a Greek German American, I can tell you that I personally have an ongoing love affair with food! When I was a kid, our home's heartbeat could be found in the kitchen. The aroma of home greeted anyone walking into the back lawn of my parents' home. My father associated love and care with food and never allowed someone to come to our home and not eat! I've carried that tradition on in my own home as well.

As Christians, our very existence and promise is birthed and centered in food and drink. Jesus was the sacrificial lamb. His human body was broken and His precious aromatic blood spilled in honor of *God's* promises and our redemption. Truly the love meal of life.

We are invited daily to His precious meal to sup with Him (Those) who created us (Gen. 1:31). While the bedazzle of a sexy life filled with busyness and gain, autonomy, technology, dating, and self-knowledge may entice us singles to think that the meal of Jesus isn't entirely fulfilling, it is my hope, as your hostess and proverbial chef, that in the sharing of this meal, you have discovered or been strengthened in your place at the aromatic, satiating, and all-satisfying table of life.

While we have shared this dining experience together, it doesn't mean that your usual human hunger pangs won't resurface in the way of feeling lonely, forgotten, or frustrated. But I'm believing that in those moments, the mind of Christ in you will recall the words of life that you find here and will rise to scatter your enemies of comparison, despair, striving, and hopelessness (see Ps. 68:1). These words will serve you, helping you keep your virtue, tend to the garden of your heart, and continue to see yourself—and treat yourself—as the valuable bride-to-be of Christ that you *are*.

I hope that the words of truth contained in this meal will also serve as a weapon in those times when the enemy of your soul comes in like a flood and you are tempted to throw in the towel of holiness for his meal of slop.

The meal that you have just partaken of is entirely subjective from the experiential standpoint—it was crafted in the kitchen of my own life. But as you made your way through the accompanying Scriptures, I pray that He has met you exactly where *you* are within your own story.

It was with the humble curiosity of a child mixed with wounds from the world and from sin that I encountered my Fiancé in the truths that I have recorded on these pages. *He* graciously and abundantly met me, and as He fragmented my life's hard drive, I realized that I was complete in Him by His Spirit. And so are you.

I have written to share our story. His and mine. And possibly yours.

You have not sat at this table by coincidence. I don't believe in it. Our days are in God's hands (see Ps. 31), and He makes provision for us in our desert places (see Isa. 43:19). He shows up at the soured wells of our lives to offer us another chance of accepting, growing, and rising—rising to become what we already are in and through Jesus Christ.

Satisfied in Him

As I have come to know Jesus on a new level of salvation, friendship, and lordship, He has been kind enough to reveal more of myself to me. So often as singles we hope that our circle will become complete when that godly mate we are waiting on drops from the sky—that somehow we will know more about ourselves when someone else arrives on the scene. While marriage certainly reveals and shapes more of who we are and can be, our lives are completely full in Him and can be revealed and lived as passionately and completely as any married couple and in many ways, more so. After all, the One who reveals us to ourselves isn't a man but the God who carefully knitted us in our mothers' womb. Who better to show us how majestically awesome we are than the One who knew us first?

As I wrote this to you, several thoughts occurred to me about what I was calling others to join me in accomplishing in life: One, I can't make it through what I'm calling other ladies to alone. Won't happen. My life, holistically, is not complete without my sisters running with me. And two, men are not our problem or solution.

Trying to reconcile who we are and what our truth is in these days of fifty-one shades of cray is challenging, to say the least, but thankfully God never changes, and neither does His Word. Let's face it, the race we run today isn't the same one our sisters in Jesus' time ran. They were matched and married by twelve or thirteen. Yep, right about hormone rage time, they were entering the tent with their young husbands and starting life as a new family. But seriously.

Now, however, we have the raging hormones from twelve to death, and are told to still live holy. Yeah, *that's* easy. We have the same desires for a mate that Mary or Martha did (unless we buy the idea that we shouldn't be so needy when it comes to an innocent God-given desire to share our lives with someone), but now we live a little longer than those ladies did (a lot longer in most cases), often without that lifelong mate. Oh sure, we might have mates, but with some of them we end up like spiritual, emotional, and physical Rahabs or, my personal inspiration for this book, our lady at the well (see John 4:10).

Thankfully, though, while God has not changed and still calls us to holiness because we are His and because He is holy, in His infinite grace He has provided completion for us in Christ that trumps all culture, physiology, or ideology. While this doesn't always seem exciting (I can feel the eye rolls as you read this; heck, mine half roll typing it), it's only because our flesh wants to think that Jesus in not enough. But the Spirit knows better. It *is* totally possible for us to live complete, joy-filled lives while waiting for or even without ever having a mate.

My absolute hope for you, now that you have shared in the meal that is this book, is that you will discover that the areas in your life that are not illuminated can only be filled by *you* partnering with *Him*. I hope that you will *glow* everywhere your feet tread, beginning where you stand in front of your own mirror, and that by the time a man finds you, if that's in your future, you will know you are a blessing, he will know he's been blessed, and your generations will rise up and call you blessed.

My Prayer for You

I have prayed for you, that in whatever snare has caught you or whatever sifting you are currently weathering, He will keep you, that your faith will not fail, and that after you recover yourself (see Luke 22:31–32), you will restore your sisters (sound familiar?). Beginning with your daughters, if you have them. This is His will for you.

Whether you are naked and torn or fully clothed in religion, I pray that the meal you have partaken of in the pages of this book will feed those malnourished and parched places in you that only His Spirit can reach.

I pray that every cell of your being rises up and stands to serve you in truth. Because the truth came to serve and save us, not condemn us (John 13:16). I pray that your mind is renewed (see Rom. 12:2) and your parched and withered hearts are watered. I pray that the hope and joy of your salvation are renewed (see Ps. 51:12) in a deepened and enlarged way. As your heart enlarges, I pray that his statutes (see Ps. 119:68) become yours so that you can live the beautifully whole (perfected) life that He planned for you from the foundations of the earth (see Jer. 1:5).

I pray sobriety, peace, and love over you today and every day. We women are so proud of being working ladies—so let's work *this* (see Phil. 2:12).

I pray that those of you eating this meal alone will be a "safe place" for yourself and that you will receive revelation and healing for your life without accusation, fear, or doubt. I pray that those of you in groups will create places of safety for each other where confidentiality is top priority, and I pray that you will take seriously the call to cover each other in love without judgment and condemnation.

This is our kingdom's way. Let it be so with us.

My mother. She has single handedly made me the feminine woman I am. The embodiment of courage and femininity, Helga blessed me with a passion for the beauty of making things beautiful, an understanding that making a home begins with me, and caring for all the dainty parts of me as a woman. She took the shame and apologies out of being beautiful as I watched her embrace and share her beauty with the world.

My sweet father. A WWII vet and lifelong GM employee, he taught me how to work hard, how to forgive and forgive often, savor life, embrace my calling and extend love through every homemade meal.

My daughter, Bean. The Princess of my life, she is best part of me and my greatest accomplishment to date. She is the light of God's heart & the reason I breathed for many years.

My lifelong friend, Pano. Having been raised in the Greek Orthodox community of Atlanta, I invited Chef Pano Karatassos to this meal for his passion and love of all things delicious. A fellow artist, he delivers an exquisite cuisine with the love of a servant's heart and the soul of a passionate visionary.

I can't possibly thank every person who has joined this journey with me, but here are a few . . . .

Thank you to the following ladies who helped me with this vision and proved to be wise counsel: Ali, Staci, Audra, Sheryl, Stephanie, Valerie, Amy & Laura

Thank you Scott Slade, my mentor and great friend. Your encouraging belief in my faith, talents and gifts has brought me to a new level of 'integration' I could not have imagined or realized, without you.

Thank you to my fellow creatives and visionaries, Bill Blankschaen and his StoryBuilders team (Faith, Sarah, Branden, and Jen) for making this birthing process exciting, cohesive and professional on every level. Thank you Rob for sharing your gift of design and PATIENCE.

To my faithful friends: Stewart, Staci, Leigh, Greg, Laura, Chantelle, Meghan, Doug, Sheryl, Garic, Pano, Paula, Sandy, Wendy, Jeff, Perry & Bella, thank you for your investment in all things Monica in more ways than one, I'm so grateful. You've enabled me to feed the Kingdom and for that, I ask God to bless you, abundantly.

LET'S STAY IN TOUCH!

I hope you've enjoyed our "meal" together as much as I've enjoyed preparing it for you. I invite you to visit me at my digital home online and stay connected at MonicaMatthews.com.

You can sample my music, listen to my show, and get my latest thoughts on life's craziness.

You'll find encouragement to live in the freedom Christ has won for you—and I'm usually giving away helpful resources you can use... so what have you got to lose?

If this book has helped you on your journey, I'd love to hear about it. Visit me online at MonicaMatthews.com and drop me a note.

You are NOT alone! I look forward to hearing from you!!

XO

Monica

Endnotes

Course 1: The Starting Point: Who Am I?

1. Definition of "fearfully," Brown-Driver-Briggs (Old Testament Hebrew-English Lexicon), Strong's 3372, http://lexiconcordance.com/hebrew/3372.html.
2. Definition of "wonderfully," Brown-Driver-Briggs (Old Testament Hebrew-English Lexicon), Strong's 6395, http://lexiconcordance.com/hebrew/6395.html.
3. Definition of "marvelous," Brown-Driver-Briggs (Old Testament Hebrew-English Lexicon), Strong's 6381, http://lexiconcordance.com/hebrew/6381.html.
4. Dr. Henry Wright, "Be in Health," http://www.beinhealth.com/public/?theme=bih_r1.

Course 3: Cycles of Whoredom

1. Definition of "lust," Thayer's (New Testament Greek-English Lexicon), Strong's 1937, http://lexiconcordance.com/greek/1937.html.
2. Definition of "breath" (i.e., "animal life," "sensuous nature") Thayer's (New Testament Greek-English Lexicon), Strong's 5591, http://lexiconcordance.com/greek/5591.html.

Course 4: Addicted to Love

1. Salynn Boyles, "Romantic Love Affects Your Brain Like a Drug," WebMD, October 13, 2010, http://www.webmd.com/pain-management/news/20101013/romantic-love-affects-your-brain-like-a-drug.
2. Nora Volknow, "The Essence of Drug Addiction," National Institute on Drug Abuse, http://www.denalihealthcaremi.com/develop-drug-addiction/.
3. "Habits: How They Form and How to Break Them," March 5, 2012, NPR, http://www.npr.org/2012/03/05/147192599/habits-how-they-form-and-how-to-break-them.
4. Kristina Fiore, "Addictions, Bad Habits Can 'Highjack' Brain," ABC, January 31, 2010, http://abcnews.go.com/GMA/MindMoodNews/addictions-hardwired-brain/story?id=9699738.
5. For more info on spirit beings and spiritual warfare, visit Be in Health, "Advanced Insights—Spirit World Realities and Separation," http://www.beinhealth.com/public/programs/advanced-insights.
6. WIC card—Women, Children, and Infants program benefits card.

Dessert: Celebrate!

1. 1. Wright, "Be in Health.